£7-95

Bour
D1077374

AS/A-LEVEL

Business
Studies

Malcolm Surridge

ESSENTIAL WORD
DICTIONARY

For my father, Alan Surridge, with love and gratitude.
They are not long, the days of wine and roses
out of a misty dream
our path emerges for a while, then closes.

Philip Allan Updates
Market Place
Deddington
Oxfordshire
OX15 0SE

tel: 01869 338652
fax: 01869 337590
e-mail: sales@philipallan.co.uk
www.philipallan.co.uk

RF 055891
250901
(R650)

ISBN 0 86003 376 7

Acknowledgements
I am grateful to Philip Cross for initiating this project and to Penny Fisher
for her support throughout the writing and editing stages. My thanks also
to John Wolinski for reading the manuscript and offering suggestions,
improving the final version in many ways. I am especially grateful to
Jackie for her love, support and smiles. The encouragement of a loving
wife was an essential element in writing this dictionary.

Printed by Raithby, Lawrence & Co Ltd, Leicester

Introduction

A clear understanding of the language of business is an important asset to anyone following a course in business studies. This is particularly true of students taking AS and A2 business studies. The benefits of mastering business terminology are:

- the ability to respond effectively to the many examination questions calling for definitions
- the capacity to write more authoritative and convincing answers to essays, case studies and other questions requiring extended responses
- saving of time in examinations through the use of precise language rather than lengthy and vague explanations

This dictionary contains most of the essential words and phrases you are likely to require in your AS and A2 business studies course. To make it easy to use, each entry has a standard format. First there is a simple definition. This is followed by a fuller explanation of the term. An example is then given whenever appropriate. Finally, some entries have examiner's tips. These are intended to improve your examination performance by highlighting common misunderstandings and errors as well as giving examples of good examination technique.

As a tool for learning, this dictionary can be used in a number of ways:

- To define key terms needed for answering all types of questions set at AS and A2. This might prove particularly useful when writing coursework.
- To investigate individual topic areas such as macroeconomics or sources of finance. By using the book's extensive cross-referencing (cross-references are *italicised*), it is possible to link together the key terms relating to an individual topic. Thus the entry 'sources of finance' offers links to *overdrafts, trade credit, shares* and *mortgages*. These provide further cross-references to *capital, dividends* and *cash flow*.
- As a revision aid. A list of the key AS terms is provided on pages 171–174. All other terms in this dictionary are essential for study at A2. Search for these words and phrases. Learn the simple definitions and examples and make sure you understand the terms. And finally, do not forget the examiner's tips. Success in business studies examinations is not just about subject knowledge. It is important to use your knowledge effectively to maximise the number of marks you achieve.

However you choose to use this dictionary, I hope you enjoy your course in business studies — and good luck with your examinations.

above the line: marketing term referring to promotional expenditure using independent media such as television and newspapers.

■ Above-the-line *promotion* primarily relates to advertising through a medium over which a business has no direct control. It allows businesses to reach large target audiences and is commonly used to encourage sales of consumer products. Most promotion in the UK is above the line. Above-the-line promotion is in contrast to *below-the-line* promotion.

■ *TIP* Some textbooks use the term 'above the line' to refer to an item in a firm's profit and loss account that is everyday expenditure or income rather than an unusual or exceptional item. However, this is a less common use of the phrase at AS and A2.

absenteeism: when an employee is not present at his or her work.

■ Absenteeism occurs for a variety of reasons, including sickness and industrial injury. The term is often used to describe circumstances in which an employee is absent from work frequently and without good reason. In this way, it is used as a measure of the morale and *motivation* of a workforce. High levels of absenteeism can dramatically increase a business's costs.

absorption costing: entails allocating all the costs associated with a business to some aspect of the business's operations — this might be a department, a division, a factory or a product.

■ It is normal to allocate *direct costs* in this way, but under this system *overheads* are divided up and allocated to the various aspects of the business as well. Thus a business manufacturing three products might allocate the rent of the factory, the costs of maintenance and the wages of the administration staff as part of the process of absorption costing. Using such a technique allows managers to make a judgement as to whether an individual product (or factory or division) is generating a profit.

■ *TIP* It is important to understand the advantages and disadvantages of financial techniques such as absorption costing. These provide the basic information to use when assessing the value of the technique in a business studies examination.

ACAS: see *Advisory, Conciliation and Arbitration Service*.

a

accountability: an employee's responsibility to complete particular tasks to a satisfactory standard.

■ An employee is normally accountable to a person holding a more senior position within an organisation. There has been a trend in many organisations to make employees more accountable for their actions through techniques such as *delayering, empowerment* and *delegation.*

accounting period: a period of time to which a business's accounts relate.

■ This is normally a period of 1 year, but it can, in some circumstances, be longer or shorter. Thus it is usual for a business to calculate its costs and revenues (in its *profit and loss account*) for a period of 12 months, but extending the period can make the profit look larger. Similarly, cutting the accounting period short might allow some heavy expenditure to appear in the following year's accounts.

■ *TIP* When considering and analysing sets of accounts, check the period of time they cover. Apparently healthy profit figures might not be so impressive once you realise that they cover a 15-month period!

acid test ratio: measures a business's *liquidity* (and hence its ability to pay its bills) by comparing short-term debts (or *current liabilities*) to the *liquid assets* available to the business.

■ Liquid assets include cash, money in the bank and money owed by customers. The formula for the acid test ratio is:

$$\text{acid test ratio} = \frac{\text{liquid assets}}{\text{current liabilities}}$$

The answer is expressed as a number or a ratio. A satisfactory figure is 1.1 or 1.1:1, although certain businesses (e.g. supermarkets) might operate with a lower figure.

■ *TIP* As with all ratios, it is not sufficient to know the formula; you need to have some appreciation of what the answer means, and of a 'normal' or expected value.

adding value: the process of increasing the worth or value of some resources by working on them.

■ The value of a newly manufactured product is greater than the raw materials that were put into it. The process of manufacturing has resulted in added value. Firms normally seek to maximise added value, either by minimising costs or by selling for the highest possible price as a means of maximising profits.

■ *e.g.* Some breweries add value to their products by creating theme pubs. This enables them to charge high prices for their products (beer, other drinks and meals) as consumers consider them to be of higher value.

advertising: communicating with potential customers using recognised media.

■ Firms advertise to keep existing customers loyal and to attempt to win additional customers. In some circumstances, advertising can be *informative* (e.g. when a new product is launched). At other times, it might be *persuasive* in an effort to win customers from rival firms and products.

■ *e.g.* Advertising can take a variety of forms. These include posters, as well as adverts in newspapers and magazines, on television and radio, and more recently on the Internet. The following diagram shows UK advertising expenditure in 1999.

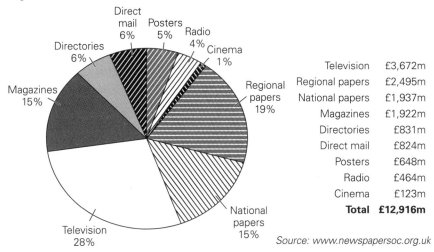

Television	£3,672m
Regional papers	£2,495m
National papers	£1,937m
Magazines	£1,922m
Directories	£831m
Direct mail	£824m
Posters	£648m
Radio	£464m
Cinema	£123m
Total	**£12,916m**

Source: www.newspapersoc.org.uk

■ *TIP* Students often think that marketing is mainly advertising, but firms engage in many other marketing activities, such as *public relations, sponsorship* and *direct mail.*

advertising elasticity: measures the responsiveness of the demand for a product to changes in the amount spent *advertising* it.

■ Advertising elasticity is measured by the formula:

$$\text{advertising elasticity} = \frac{\%\text{ change in demand for a product}}{\%\text{ change in advertising expenditure for that product}}$$

Advertising elasticity is one technique by which businesses can judge the success of their advertising campaigns. If the figure resulting from this calculation is significantly greater than 1, it tells managers that the percentage increase in demand is greater than the percentage increase in advertising expenditure that provoked it. In these circumstances, advertising might be considered effective in influencing consumers' purchasing decisions.

Advertising Standards Authority (ASA): organisation established with the task of ensuring that non-broadcast advertisements appearing in the UK are 'legal, decent, honest and truthful'.

■ The Authority, set up in 1962, protects the public by ensuring that the rules stated in the British Codes of Advertising and Sales Promotion are followed by everyone who prepares and publishes advertisements. The ASA is independent of the advertising industry and government. Its work is funded by a small levy on display advertising and direct mail expenditure. See *Code of Advertising Practice.*

a

Advisory, Conciliation and Arbitration Service (ACAS): independent and impartial organisation established to prevent and resolve industrial disputes.

■ ACAS was created by the government in 1975 to provide advice on industrial relations matters to all interested parties and to seek actively to resolve disputes through the use of *arbitration* and *conciliation*. ACAS also investigates individual cases where discrimination or *unfair dismissal* is alleged to have taken place.

AGM: see *annual general meeting*.

AIDA: stands for Awareness, Interest, Desire and Action and shows the stages a purchaser passes through before reaching a decision.

■ The model was developed in 1925 and is used to assess the preparedness of buyers to purchase a product.

■ *TIP* A number of similar models exist, charting the process of buyers from first awareness to purchase, but AIDA is probably the best known.

AIM: see *Alternative Investment Market*.

Alternative Investment Market (AIM): a UK stock exchange for smaller, growing companies that might not be eligible for a full listing on the *Stock Exchange*.

■ AIM operates under less rigorous rules than the full Stock Exchange. It was launched in 1975 and by 2000 over 400 companies from all sectors of the economy traded their shares on the market. AIM represents an efficient means by which growing companies can raise funds to continue their development. More than 70 companies have progressed from AIM to a full listing on the Stock Exchange.

amalgamation: see *integration*.

amortisation: reduction in value of *intangible assets* such as *goodwill* and *brands* over a period of time.

■ This is a form of *depreciation*, whereby the value of the asset declines through the passing of time.

■ *e.g.* A firm might hold a *patent* granting it the sole right to produce a given product for a period of 15 years. At the end of the patent's life it has no value. As the patent falls in value, it is subject to amortisation.

annual general meeting (AGM): annual meeting to which all *shareholders* are invited and at which the company presents its *annual report and accounts*, *directors* are elected and *dividends* are agreed.

■ AGMs offer shareholders the opportunity to express their views on the performance of the board of directors and to vote directors out if their achievements are considered unsatisfactory. Companies are legally obliged to hold such meetings.

■ *TIP* AGMs are not usually attended by the majority of shareholders (especially individuals who have bought shares), so they provide only a limited constraint on the activities of boards of directors.

annualised hours: stating of an employee's hours of duty on an annual rather than a weekly basis.

■ Annualised hours offer businesses greater flexibility in the use of labour, as workers can be available for busy periods without incurring extra wage costs in the form of *overtime*. Workers receive time off in compensation during quieter periods. This form of contract is widely used in seasonal businesses such as agriculture.

▨ *e.g.* Under an annualised hours contract, an agricultural worker might be required to work 700 hours over a year, rather than 35 hours each week, to allow for peak periods such as harvesting.

annual report and accounts: yearly report provided by all companies in which the financial performance of the business is recorded.

▨ It is normal for annual reports and accounts to include a copy of the *balance sheet, profit and loss account* and (for larger companies) a sources and uses of funds statement, as well as a report by the directors on the company's performance during the preceding year. Most companies use this document for public relations purposes and produce a glossy brochure highlighting the business's achievements. A copy of the annual report and accounts is sent to each shareholder prior to the company's *annual general meeting*.

Ansoff's matrix: framework employed to assist in devising a business's *marketing strategy*.

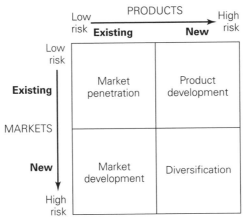

▨ The theme underlying strategies developed from Ansoff's matrix is *growth* — in a company and its sales. The matrix assists a firm in determining whether to develop new products or to expand sales of existing products, and whether to aim at increasing sales in current markets or attempt to break into new ones.

anti-competitive activity: any action by a firm that restricts or eliminates free and fair competition within a market.

▨ Such activities limit the ability of rivals to supply products to customers on an equal footing. The *Competition Commission* and the *Office of Fair Trading* oversee the operation of fair competition within the UK, although EU legislation is becoming increasingly important.

▨ *e.g.* exclusive dealing, whereby producers will only sell to retailers who agree to stock just their goods and not those of rivals. In 2000, allegations were made that the high street store Dixons and two computer manufacturers had reached an exclusive deal.

appraisal: evaluation of an individual employee's performance over a period of time.

■ Appraisal operates with the intention of improving the employee's performance in the workplace. It can be judgemental, involving an assessment of the employee's achievements against agreed targets. A proportion of the employee's pay might be linked to the achievement of appraisal targets. Other firms operate developmental appraisal systems, designed to identify and meet employees' training needs. Some managers argue that this is the most effective way to use appraisal to improve the performance of the workforce.

■ *TIP* The type of appraisal that a business uses is likely to reflect its leadership style and culture. Exploring such links can form a useful line of analysis.

appropriation account: section of the *profit and loss account* that details the uses to which profits have been put.

■ The appropriation account is normally found at the bottom of the profit and loss account and records whether profits have been paid to shareholders in the form of *dividends* or retained within the business for future investment. See also *retained profit*.

arbitration: attempt to settle an industrial dispute through the intervention of a neutral third party.

■ Arbitration is often used as a final resort when other methods have failed. It can take the form of a proposed settlement for the two parties to consider. *Binding arbitration* is more decisive, as both sides agree to accept the decision of the arbitrator. In this way, all parties can be confident that a solution will be found. Some businesses insist that disputes are automatically referred to arbitration after a certain time to avoid protracted wrangling.

arrears: overdue debts.

■ By going into arrears a *debtor* allows the due date for payment to pass by without taking action. This might be inadvertent or it might be a means of improving *cash flow* by delaying payment and retaining the cash within the business for a longer period. Over the last few years, the UK government has criticised large firms for deliberately withholding payment from smaller suppliers to improve their cash flow.

■ *TIP* Arrears are not an ethical method of improving cash flow and should not be confused with *trade credit*, which is agreed by both parties in advance.

Articles of Association: internal arrangements under which a *company* should operate.

■ Articles of Association are drawn up (along with the *Memorandum of Association*) when a company is formed. The Articles lay down the rights of shareholders and the powers of directors as well as the rules governing formal company meetings such as the *annual general meeting*. The *Registrar of Companies* holds a copy of the Articles of Association for every company at Companies House.

ASA: see *Advertising Standards Authority*.

assembly line: see *production line*.

asset: something owned by a business.

▨ Assets can be classified as current and fixed. Businesses should hold both. *Current assets* are liquid (e.g. cash) and allow a business to settle its debts as they become due. *Fixed assets* (e.g. factories, vehicles) allow a business to generate an income and to earn profits. Most assets are *tangible*, having a physical existence (e.g. vehicles, factories). Other assets are *intangible* (e.g. *goodwill, brands*). Businesses need to hold a range of assets.

asset-led marketing: entails a company using its *assets* as a central part of its *marketing strategy*.

▨ A business can use a well-known brand name or employ a major *tangible asset* that it owns as an important aspect of its marketing.

▨ *e.g.* The Virgin Group engages in asset-led marketing by using its brand name on all its products. Gleneagles Golf Club in Scotland has built a luxury hotel on the course, drawing not just on the name Gleneagles, but also on the beautiful area in which the golf club is located.

assets employed: value of all the *assets* used by a business after deducting its short-term or *current liabilities*.

▨ This is an important figure on a business's *balance sheet* as it measures the resources available to the firm. In general, higher levels of assets employed would be expected to generate higher profit levels.

▨ *TIP* Assets employed are listed on the balance sheet as total assets less current liabilities.

asset stripping: purchase of a business with the intention of breaking it up and selling the more valuable elements.

▨ Assets strippers purchase firms to resell part or all of the business rather than operating it as a continuing enterprise. Firms are vulnerable to asset stripping if the value of their *shares* is lower than the value of the *assets* held by the business.

asset turnover: ratio of a business's *sales* to the *assets* available to it.

▨ The formula to calculate this ratio is:

$$\text{asset turnover} = \frac{\text{sales}}{\text{net assets}}$$

This formula measures the efficiency with which businesses use their assets. An increasing ratio over time generally indicates that a firm is operating with greater efficiency. A fall in the ratio can be caused by a decline in sales or an increase in *assets employed*. Asset turnover ratios vary enormously.

▨ *e.g.* A supermarket might have a high figure as it has relatively few assets in relation to sales. A shipbuilding firm is likely to have a much lower ratio because it requires many more assets to engage in production.

assisted areas: specific parts of the UK selected to receive financial support from the UK and EU authorities.

■ Firms locating to, or operating in, the areas shown in the map below might receive aid as part of the government's *regional policy*. The aim of regional policy is to regenerate areas that have been subject to economic decline. Grants are awarded to firms with the intention of promoting prosperity and improving the competitiveness of local businesses. A number of forms of financial support are available (e.g. regional selective assistance).

☐ Assisted area

Source: www.dti.gov.uk

audit: detailed inspection of the financial accounts of a company by qualified and independent persons.

■ Audits are normally conducted annually to ensure that the business's financial records give a 'true and fair view' of the state of the business. Auditors report to the shareholders of the company, although smaller companies are exempt from audit requirements.

■ *TIP* Many businesses conduct audits (or independent investigations) into other areas of their activities. Audits into environmental performance and the impact of a business on society are becoming increasingly common. See *environmental audit* and *social audit*.

authorised share capital (also called 'registered capital' or 'nominal capital')**:** maximum amount of *capital* that a company is allowed to raise through the sale of *shares*.

■ The company cannot exceed this amount, although it might choose not to raise all the capital to which it is entitled. The authorised share capital is stated in the company's *Articles of Association* and can only be altered by application to the *Registrar of Companies*. See also *issued capital*.

authoritarian leadership: style whereby the leader keeps control of information and makes the major decisions alone.

■ This style of *leadership* sets objectives and retains control at all times. The leader will use one-way communication and give little authority to junior employees. This style can be useful when quick decisions are required and it leads to consistent decision making. However, it is unlikely to develop or motivate subordinates.

■ *TIP* It is often useful to link leadership style to *McGregor*'s theories. McGregor analysed how a leader's perception of his or her workforce shapes the style in which the leader operates. An authoritarian leader is likely to hold a *Theory X* view of the workforce.

autonomous working groups: teams which are given a high level of control over their working lives.

■ Senior managers delegate considerable authority to those further down the hierarchy, allowing them to decide what tasks to complete at what times and giving them some control over the resources available to the group. In some cases, autonomous working groups elect their own leader and appoint new staff. The intention behind the creation of such groups is to improve *motivation* and *productivity*. Such an approach is unlikely to succeed without careful preparation and significant amounts of training.

■ *e.g.* Honda at Swindon makes use of autonomous working groups.

average: method of calculating a single number to represent the central value of a set of numbers.

■ The *mean* is the most common form of the average and is calculated by adding together all the numbers in the set and dividing the result by the number of items in the set.

■ *e.g.* A firm's monthly sales (£m) for the first 4 months of the year are as follows:

	(£m)
January	125
February	146
March	149
April	160

Total sales over the 4 months were £580 million, giving an average monthly sales figure (580/4) of £145 million.

■ *TIP* Other methods of calculating a single figure to represent a group of data include the mode (the most common value) and the median (the middle value when the data are assembled in order).

a

average cost: see *unit cost*.

average fixed costs: *fixed costs* of a business divided by the level of output of that business.

■ Fixed costs do not alter as the firm increases its output (at least in the short run), so average fixed costs fall continuously as output increases. Firms therefore seek to produce the highest possible output from their resources, so that average fixed costs are minimised. This allows prices to be lowered or higher profits to be enjoyed.

average rate of return: method of assessing the worth of an *investment* by calculating the yearly percentage return on the sum invested.

■ The calculation uses the formula below:

$$\text{average rate of return} = \frac{\text{average annual profit}}{\text{initial investment}} \times 100$$

Average annual profit is calculated by dividing the total profit from an investment by the number of years to which the profit relates. The average rate of return allows managers to compare alternative investments as well as to contrast the percentage rate of return with that available from investing in financial institutions. Because this technique calculates an average figure for profits, it ignores the timing of payments. Most firms would prefer to receive higher profits in the years immediately following the investment.

backward vertical integration: joining together of one firm with another which is in the same industry, but at an earlier stage of production.

■ Such *integration* offers the benefits of secure markets to the firm at the earlier stage in the production process and assured supplies to the other firm. It can also allow savings by linking together production, possibly permitting the use of *just-in-time* stock systems and reducing the costs of holding stocks.

■ *e.g.* the takeover of a hop-growing farm by a brewery.

bad debt: money owed by customers which is most unlikely to be recovered by a business.

■ Bad debts are a particular problem for a business offering large amounts of *trade credit*. While this approach might stimulate sales, it also increases the risk of the business not receiving payment. Bad debts are a normal business expense and appear on the *profit and loss account*. An effective system of credit control is a means of reducing bad debts. This requires careful assessment of customers before offering any credit, and chasing up of debts as soon as they become overdue.

balance of payments: record of a country's trading and financial transactions with the rest of the world over a stated period of time.

■ The balance of payments is data collected and published by the government and is an important element in the management of the economy by the UK authorities. It includes data on exports and *imports* of goods (visibles) and services (invisibles). The authorities aim to balance earnings from exports with expenditure on imports. The balance of payments also records investment by foreigners in the UK and investment by UK citizens and firms overseas.

balance of trade: financial record of a country's trade in goods, specifically manufactured goods, with the rest of the world over a stated period of time.

■ It is normal for the balance of trade only to include transactions in goods (*visible trade*) and to exclude services. The UK traditionally has a deficit on its balance of trade as it excludes sales of services overseas, such as banking, insurance and tourism.

■ *TIP* It is easy to make an error and assume that the balance of trade includes trade in services (invisibles). In fact these are excluded from the account.

balance sheet: financial statement recording the *assets* and *liabilities* of a business at the end of an *accounting period*.

▦ The balance sheet is the primary financial document published by businesses and is conventionally set out as shown below.

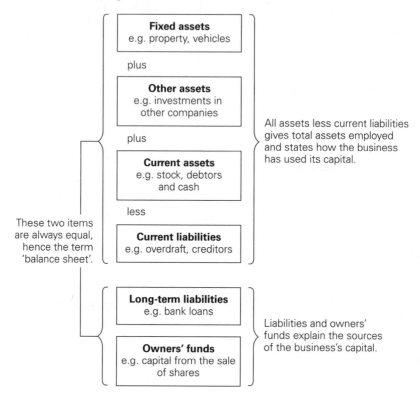

These two items are always equal, hence the term 'balance sheet'.

Fixed assets
e.g. property, vehicles

plus

Other assets
e.g. investments in other companies

plus

Current assets
e.g. stock, debtors and cash

less

Current liabilities
e.g. overdraft, creditors

All assets less current liabilities gives total assets employed and states how the business has used its capital.

Long-term liabilities
e.g. bank loans

Owners' funds
e.g. capital from the sale of shares

Liabilities and owners' funds explain the sources of the business's capital.

▦ By recording assets and liabilities, the balance sheet sets out the ways in which a business has raised its capital and the uses to which this capital has been put. The balance sheet provides a great deal of information for those with an interest in a business, especially providing important data allowing *ratio analysis* to be carried out.

Bank of England: the central bank of the UK, offering banking and other financial services to the government and other financial institutions.

▦ The Bank was established in 1694 and is located in Threadneedle Street in the heart of the City of London. The Bank has many roles: since 1997 its Monetary Policy Committee has set interest rates in order to meet the government's inflation target; it raises money for the government by selling its stock and bonds; it issues the country's bank notes. It collects and publishes financial and banking data in order to monitor developments in the UK's financial system. However, the Bank is no longer responsible for the day-to-day supervision of other financial institutions.

bank rate: see *base rate*.

bankruptcy: when an individual or *unincorporated* firm is judged to be unable to pay its debts by a court of law.

▨ In these circumstances, the *assets* of the individual or business will be sold and the proceeds raised will be shared between those who are owed money (*creditors*). Firms or individuals can elect to become voluntarily bankrupt or might be forced into bankruptcy by creditors.

▨ *TIP* A common mistake among students is to refer to companies 'being made bankrupt'. Companies cannot become bankrupt; they are subject to *liquidation*.

bar chart: method of presenting numerical data using a chart with horizontal or vertical bars.

▨ A bar chart gives readers an immediate overall impression of data, some of which might be complex. Bar charts are particularly useful for making comparisons. However, it is difficult to read figures precisely, and altering the scale of the chart can alter the overall visual impression.

▨ *e.g.* The following bar chart shows British car production in 1999.

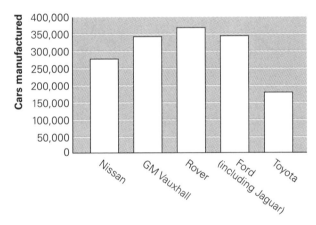

▨ *TIP* When reading bar charts, check the scale on the y-axis (the vertical axis). Differences or changes in data can be exaggerated by excluding much of the range of the data. In our example above, we could have highlighted Toyota's small production level by starting the axis at 150,000 cars per year.

barriers to entry: obstacles imposed by established firms making it difficult (or impossible) for new firms to enter the market.

▨ Barriers to entry are most common in oligopolistic markets, where relatively few large firms are in competition. See *oligopoly*.

▨ *e.g.* lowering prices to levels that new firms find difficult to match, engaging in major promotional campaigns, restricting access to essential raw materials or other resources, and emphasising *product differentiation* to encourage *brand loyalty*.

barter: direct exchange (or swapping) of one item for another without using money as a medium of exchange.

▨ Barter is traditionally associated with subsistence economies that have not developed a monetary system. It is an inefficient system of exchange because it requires the matching of wants for two people. Not only is it necessary to find a person who wants what you have to offer, but also you need to desire what he or she is offering in exchange. This 'double coincidence of wants' is not always easy to achieve.

base rate (also called 'bank rate'): rate of interest set by the Monetary Policy Committee of the *Bank of England*.

This is the rate upon which all other *interest rates* are based. Thus rates charged by banks, building societies and those existing in the financial markets vary directly with the base rate. The Monetary Policy Committee meets each month to determine the rate of interest. Recent governments have used the rate of interest as a major method of controlling the economy.

batch production: type of *production* in which groups of items move through the stages of production at the same time.

Batch production allows businesses to use their equipment for a variety of purposes, making efficient use of what might be expensive resources. It is also commonly used by businesses in response to the receipt of a specific order.

e.g. This approach to production is used in industries such as baking, where a batch of one type of bread or cakes is produced together to be followed by a different product.

below the line: range of promotional activities over which the firm has some control.

In contrast to *above-the-line* promotion, below-the-line promotion does not entail the use of independent media such as television or newspapers; nor does it normally involve the payment of a fee to an advertising agency.

e.g. sponsorship, trade promotions, *merchandising* and *public relations*.

benchmarking: process of comparing products or production processes against those judged to be the best in the industry.

Managers implement benchmarking to learn from the excellence of other firms and improve their own performance. Benchmarking requires that firms observe the products or processes of others before implementing change in their own organisation (including training) to reach the same standards of performance. It should be a continuous process because levels of performance regularly improve.

TIP It is important to remember that much benchmarking relates to all aspects of a business's activities (customer services, delivery on time, etc.) rather than just to the quality of the end product.

binding arbitration: type of *arbitration* whereby the parties agree to accept the decision of the arbitrator, whatever the outcome.

Binding arbitration ensures that an agreement is reached and can bring disputes to a speedy end. However, both parties have to agree to the process and such an agreement can be difficult to achieve in a bitter or prolonged dispute.

e.g. In the case of an industrial dispute over a pay settlement, the neutral third party would consider the arguments presented by both parties to the dispute before reaching a decision, probably in the form of a percentage pay rise.

blue-chip company: well-known and respected company whose shares are considered to be a safe and reliable investment.

The term 'blue chip' originated in casinos, where blue chips are the ones with the highest monetary value.

e.g. Marks & Spencer, British Telecommunications and Shell.

blue-collar union: union representing workers who do unskilled manual tasks.

Employees who are members of blue-collar unions might work on the shop-floor completing dirty tasks requiring the wearing of overalls — it is from this that the term 'blue-collar' originated. Blue-collar unions have become less common as a result of *mergers* and *amalgamations* leading to the creation of *general unions*.

e.g. the Amalgamated Engineering Union.

board of directors: people elected by the *shareholders* of a company to manage the enterprise.

The board of directors meets regularly to determine the strategic direction of the business. Directors are elected annually at the company's *annual general meeting*. Boards of directors are made up of full-time salaried people (executive directors) and part-time directors hired for some specific knowledge or skills that they possess (non-executive directors).

Boston matrix: allows firms to classify their products according to their rate of growth and the growth of the market of which they are a part.

	MARKET GROWTH	
	High	**Low**
High	Star	Cash cow
Low	Problem child	Dog

The Boston matrix is a valuable technique by which businesses can determine their strategy concerning the development of new products. Firms should aim to have a broad portfolio of products, with some in each category of the matrix. This should ensure that the firm has a range of new and well-established products, and that it generates sufficient cash to fund the development of the newer products.

bottleneck: a factor that causes any aspect of a firm's normal trading activity to be delayed or stopped.

b

▨ Such delays might only occur at one stage in a production process, but might hold up the entire activity. The economy is also described as suffering from a bottleneck when demand for the products of one or more industries outstrips their ability to supply.

▨ *e.g.* delays in the delivery of supplies, the breakdown of essential machinery and ineffective planning by managers.

BPR: see *business process re-engineering.*

brand: name, sign, symbol or design used to differentiate a good or service from those supplied by competitors.

▨ A number of companies have recognised the value of their brand names by including them as an *asset* on their *balance sheet.*

▨ *e.g.* Coca-Cola and Microsoft have enormous value and are recognised throughout the world. Brand names have been an important issue for many financial institutions offering services via the Internet — gimmicky names such as Smile, Egg and Cahoot are gaining popularity and value.

brand leader: product or range of products that is generally considered to be the leader in its field.

▨ Firms spend large amounts of money promoting their brands with the intention of making them a leader. Brand leadership can result in higher sales and profits.

▨ *e.g.* Microsoft is undoubtedly the global brand leader for PC software.

brand loyalty: measures the strength of a consumer's preference for a particular brand.

▨ In some circumstances, brand loyalty might be so strong that consumers refuse to purchase an alternative product. Brand loyalty depends upon businesses succeeding in differentiating their products from those of their rivals. In some cases, such differentiation might be a matter of perception rather than reality. Brand loyalty helps firms to retain customers and might allow them to charge higher prices.

▨ *e.g.* In the UK, the Co-operative Bank has achieved a degree of brand loyalty by implementing a well-publicised ethical policy to differentiate its services from those of other banks.

break even: level of output at which the *revenue* earned by a firm (or one of its products) is equal to total costs of *production.*

▨ At this level of output, the firm or product makes neither a *loss* nor a *profit.* A break-even chart illustrates the costs and revenues associated with the business, and allows the level of break-even output to be determined and marked. A quicker and simpler alternative is to calculate break-even output by use of the formula below.

$$\text{break-even output} = \frac{\text{fixed costs}}{\text{selling price per unit} - \text{variable cost per unit}}$$

Break even is a useful rule of thumb, and particularly valuable for small and newly established businesses.

TIP It is important to express the result of any break-even calculation as a level of output. Break even is not a value; it is a quantity.

budget: financial plan for some specified future period of time.

Budgets can relate to the expected income or revenue of a firm, in which case they are termed 'sales budgets'. Equally, budgets can be drawn up for expenditure: a production budget is likely to record expected costs of labour, raw materials and overheads. All budgets are drawn together in the master budget, from which a firm can create a forecast *profit and loss account*. Recently, many European firms have delegated control over budgets to more junior employees as a means of motivation. See also *revenue budget*.

budgeting: drawing up financial plans and monitoring the performance of a business in attaining them.

Budgeting is an important part of financial control within an organisation. Managers use *variance* analysis as a method of comparing budgets with actual expenditure and income figures. The results of variance analysis provide important information for managers, allowing problems to be rectified and future plans and strategy to be adjusted.

buffer stocks: raw materials or finished goods kept by businesses as part of their *stock control* system to guard against supply problems or unexpected increases in demand.

Buffer stocks are the minimum level of stocks that a business considers necessary to avoid disruption to production. Some manufacturers hold buffer stocks of raw materials to ensure uninterrupted production, although modern techniques of stock management have reduced holdings. Under the system of *just-in-time* stock management, firms do not hold buffer stocks of materials or components, but rely upon deliveries arriving just as they are required. Manufacturers and retailers hold buffer stocks of finished goods to ensure that they can meet their customers' demands.

bulk buying: offers purchasers reduced prices in return for ordering large quantities.

Buyers are able to negotiate prices below the list price and extended periods of *trade credit*. It is not unusual for businesses to offer discounts for bulk purchases as a means of generating additional orders. The ability to gain discounts for bulk purchases is an example of firms benefiting from *economies of scale*.

e.g. Large retailers such as Sainsbury's and Tesco place huge orders with suppliers and have considerable bargaining power to negotiate prices downwards.

business angel: person who has a considerable personal fortune and is willing to use this money to support risky ventures.

Business angels are prepared to lend relatively small amounts of between £10,000 and £50,000 as well as larger sums and have become an important source of *venture capital*. In 1998, business angels lent nearly £25 million to UK companies. Many of these loans were made to companies in high-

b

technology industries such as computing. Business angels are an important *source of finance* for expansion of small firms and for business start-ups.

business cycle (also called 'trade cycle'): regular change in the level of national economic activity characterised by boom, *recession, slump* and upswing.

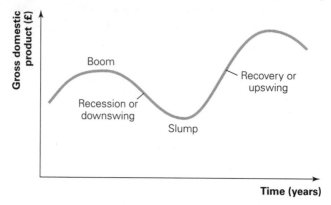

- The business cycle has significant implications for businesses, with demand for most products and services rising and falling with the level of activity in the economy. The government uses *fiscal policy* and *monetary policy* to lessen the side-effects of the business cycle.
- *e.g.* Firms selling luxury products (those with income-elastic demand) are particularly susceptible to changes in demand as the business cycle moves through its stages.

business plan: document produced by a business, especially when first established, detailing its expected activities, incomes and expenditures.

- A typical business plan will contain information on the business idea, the qualifications and experience of the manager, marketing, staff and other assets required, and cash-flow and profit forecasts. For many new businesses, such a plan is essential to test the commercial viability of a business idea and to iron out any potential problems. Most financial institutions require a business plan before they will lend money to a new enterprise. This type of plan can prove useful in assisting managers to monitor whether a business is achieving its targets.

business process re-engineering (BPR): fundamental redesign of the key processes within an organisation to achieve dramatic improvements in overall performance.

- Business process re-engineering is intended to result in lower costs, higher *productivity* and improved *customer service*. It might entail businesses making substantial capital investments to achieve large-scale improvements in productivity. BPR is likely to involve radical changes in the way a business operates, perhaps leading to new technology, new production techniques and considerable retraining. BPR leads to revolutionary change, while *kaizen* is evolutionary.

CAP: see *Code of Advertising Practice*.

capacity: maximum output a business can produce when using its factories, workforce and other resources as intensively as possible.

■ A firm's capacity can be affected by the quality of its workforce and its capital equipment as well as by the efficiency with which the management team uses the resources available to it. Businesses can increase their capacity by investing in more factory space, machinery and other physical assets, and by training the workforce to improve *productivity*. Managers are unlikely to take a decision to invest in additional capacity unless they are convinced that any increase in demand from consumers is likely to continue in the long term.

capacity shortage: where a business has insufficient resources to meet fully the demands of its customers.

■ In such circumstances, a business might lack sufficient factory space or might not have an adequate number of skilled employees. In the short term, a business might ask employees to work overtime or *subcontract* some of its work to another business. In the longer term, a firm might have to invest in acquiring more factory or office space and hiring and training additional employees.

capacity utilisation: measures the extent to which a business uses the *capacity* available to it.

■ Capacity utilisation is normally expressed in percentage terms. Thus if an Internet bank has the staff and technology to deal with 800 customers an hour on-line, but only receives an average of 600 customers, its capacity utilisation would be $600/800 \times 100 = 75\%$. Utilising capacity as fully as possible assists a business's profitability by spreading fixed costs over the highest possible level of output.

■ *TIP* This is a popular area for exam questions. In particular, you should be aware of how firms might respond to the problems associated with *excess capacity*.

capital: (1) money invested within a business in the form of *shares* and loans.

■ To commence trading and to expand its scale, a business requires an input of this form of capital. In these contexts, we would refer to start-up capital and possibly *venture capital*.

(2) value of the assets (land, property, machinery, etc.) available to a business.

■ *TIP* Students often use the term 'money' when they mean capital. Using terminology correctly in a response adds conviction to an answer.

capital budget: plan for expenditure on *fixed assets* such as property, machinery and vehicles over some future period.

■ Preparing capital budgets might involve the firm in negotiating long-term loans or issuing more shares. Capital budgets also require managers to undertake *investment appraisal* as part of the planning process. In contrast to capital budgets, *revenue budgets* are financial plans for expenditure on items such as wages and raw materials.

capital employed: total funds invested in a business.

■ This will comprise capital raised through the selling of shares as well as funds borrowed on a long-term basis. It includes *ordinary* and *preference share* capital, *reserves, debentures* and long-term loans. Capital employed is shown on the *balance sheet* as total *assets employed* and provides a clear indication of the resources available to the managers and directors of the business.

■ *TIP* The capital employed figure is used extensively in *ratio analysis* as part of the evaluation of the financial performance of a firm. By comparing profits with the capital employed, it is possible to assess the efficiency with which the business is managed.

capital expenditure: spending undertaken by a business to purchase *fixed assets* such as property, machinery and vehicles.

■ Capital expenditure normally follows some assessment of the costs of, and likely returns from, the investment through the process of *investment appraisal*. Such expenditure can place a substantial burden on a business, but it is essential if the business is to be able to generate profits. In contrast to capital expenditure, *revenue expenditure* is the purchase of everyday items such as fuel, raw materials and components.

capital goods: machinery and equipment used to produce other goods.

■ The purchase of capital goods is essential because they are used in the production of other goods. Such purchases require a business to undertake *capital expenditure*. In contrast, goods sold directly to customers are termed 'consumer goods'.

■ *e.g.* robots on production lines, lathes and delivery vehicles.

capital intensive: style of production in which firms use high proportions of capital equipment and relatively little labour.

■ Some industries (e.g. the manufacture of steel or glass) require heavy expenditure on *fixed assets* to make production possible. Steel production is not possible without blast furnaces and equipment to roll the molten metal. Thus steel manufacturers have to purchase large amounts of capital equipment before starting production. In contrast, many businesses providing services (e.g. painting and decorating) rely heavily upon *labour* and use little capital equipment in the production process. Some firms might choose to use a high proportion of technology and little labour in the production process because labour is scarce, expensive or unreliable, perhaps due to industrial relations problems.

cartel: when two or more businesses collude to control prices and/or output levels to limit competition and increase profits.

■ Cartels can operate in a number of ways. Firms can simply set a common price (above the free market price), offering consumers no choice and increasing the profits of the firms concerned. A more comprehensive form of a cartel involves coordinating output levels to restrict production and keep prices artificially high. Cartels are illegal in most advanced economies. See also *collusion*.

■ *e.g.* At times, firms providing air travel and those engaged in diamond mining have operated cartels.

cash: money in the form of notes and coins, as opposed to cheques or credit cards.

■ Cash is the most *liquid asset* that a business can hold. Businesses need to hold sufficient cash to meet day-to-day commitments (e.g. paying for supplies when credit is not available). However, firms seek to minimise holdings of cash because they do not earn any return. The development of other forms of money, particularly credit and debit cards, has resulted in less cash being used for everyday transactions.

cash cow: product holding a high share of sales in a market that is growing slowly.

■ Cash cows are one of the categories of the *Boston matrix* devised by the Boston Consulting Group. Firms require cash cows as part of their *product portfolio* for their ability to generate the high levels of cash necessary to support and develop other, less established, products in the firm's portfolio.

■ *e.g.* Philips (the Dutch electronics firm) has international cash cows in the form of lighting products and televisions that they have used to fund other product ranges, including CDs and digital compact cassettes.

cash flow: amounts of money moving into and out of a business over an *accounting period*.

■ Money flows into a business as a result of the sale of goods and services. Money from cash sales is received immediately, while if customers are given time to pay (*trade credit*) the money inflow will occur later. Expenditure on items such as raw materials, components, fuel and wages results in cash outflow. The balance between the inflow and outflow of cash over any given period is termed *net cash flow*.

■ *TIP* Cash flow and *profit* are frequently confused, but they are, in fact, very different. Profit, in its simplest sense, is the amount by which revenues exceed costs. Cash flow, on the other hand, relates to the timing of payments and receipts. Thus a profitable business might face cash-flow difficulties because, for example, customers delay payments.

cash-flow forecast: document that records a business's anticipated inflows and outflows of cash over a future *accounting period*, normally a year.

Drawing up a cash-flow forecast is an important part of financial planning for all businesses, but especially newly established ones. A cash-flow forecast identifies times at which a business might face shortages of cash and enables managers to make arrangements (e.g. the use of an *overdraft*) to overcome any difficulties. The format of a typical cash-flow forecast is set out below.

	January	February	March	April
Cash inflow				
Cash sales				
Credit sales				
Total inflow				
Cash outflow				
Raw materials				
Rent and rates				
Wages and salaries				
Other costs				
Total outflow				
Net cash flow				
Opening balance				
Closing balance				

cash-flow statement: financial statement showing the actual flows into and out of a business during an *accounting period*.

The cash-flow statement draws on information recorded in the *balance sheet* and *profit and loss account*. Conventionally, cash-flow statements comprise eight sections recording all the inflows and outflows of cash that have taken place. The cash-flow statement concentrates upon the business's *liquidity* position. A cash-flow statement can explain why, after a profitable year's trading, a business's cash position might have deteriorated. All companies (except the very smallest) are legally obliged to produce a cash-flow statement as part of their annual accounts.

CBI: see *Confederation of British Industry*.

cell production: method of *production* in which the manufacturing process is organised into independent teams (or cells), each of which produces a group (or family) of goods.

Teams of employees operating cells might be given considerable control over their working lives to improve their *motivation* and *productivity*.

e.g. Boulton and Paul, manufacturers of timber doors and windows, recorded substantial improvements in productivity as a result of using cell production.

centralisation: when an organisation is controlled by a small number of senior managers who take all the major decisions.

Such organisations make little use of *delegation*, and junior employees have limited input into the decision-making process. Centralised businesses can respond quickly to external change and take decisions rapidly. The business is also able to project a consistent image to the public. However, centralised organisations might not make the most effective use of their employees and such an approach might prove difficult to sustain as the organisation grows. See also *decentralisation*.

Chancellor of the Exchequer: the British government minister responsible for managing the economy.

■ The Chancellor decides upon the rates of *taxation* and the levels of (and targets for) *public spending*. The role also extends to overseeing the government's *regional policy, exchange rate* policy and negotiations over the UK's entry to the *European Monetary Union*. In May 1997, the government ceded control of interest rates to the Monetary Policy Committee at the *Bank of England*.

civil law: governs the legal relationships between individuals and organisations.

■ Civil law might be invoked in the case of disputes between individuals or businesses; the state is not directly involved as a prosecutor. Punishments under civil law include damages and injunctions to restrain the actions of individuals or organisations.

■ *e.g.* Disputes under civil law might occur because one party believes that a breach of contract has occurred or that negligence has taken place (possibly resulting in injury).

closed shop: arrangement whereby all employees of a business are obliged to be members of a particular *trade union*.

■ Trade unions operating closed shops used to have considerable industrial power as they controlled the entire workforce of the business. However, a series of Employment Acts during the 1980s and early 1990s made it unlawful for trade unions to insist on the operation of closed shops. In particular, the Employment Act of 1990 made it unlawful for a business not to employ an individual because he or she refused to join a trade union.

■ *e.g.* Closed shop arrangements were once common in the printing industry, acting and journalism.

Code of Advertising Practice (CAP): code operated by the *Advertising Standards Authority* with the intention of promoting 'legal, decent, honest and truthful' *advertising*.

■ This code is not legally enforceable, but firms normally respond to any request by the ASA to withdraw an advert considered to breach the code. The ASA can apply sanctions to firms that refuse to take its advice by advising the media not to carry any further adverts until the dispute is resolved.

■ *e.g.* Well-known companies such as Benetton and French Connection have been subject to action by the ASA in recent years.

collateral: form of security required by financial organisations before granting a loan.

■ This security must have significant monetary value (normally in excess of the

C

amount of the loan) and be relatively easy to convert into cash. If the person or organisation receiving the loan defaults on their payments, the collateral might be sold to repay the debt.

■ *e.g.* property and *stocks* and *shares*. Many businesses raise loans called *mortgages* by using their property as collateral.

collective bargaining: negotiation between employers and the representatives of the workforce, normally *trade union* officials.

■ These negotiations are likely to cover issues such as wages and salaries, holidays, the length of the working week and pensions. Because the negotiation is collective, any agreement that is reached applies to all members of the workforce represented at the meeting. The rules for collective bargaining are usually agreed within each individual firm as part of the process itself.

■ *TIP* The decline in the power and influence of trade unions in the latter part of the twentieth century means that collective bargaining now receives less attention from the media. However, it remains an important element of industrial relations and a valid topic for examination questions.

collusion: agreement between two or more businesses with the intention of restricting free and fair competition.

■ Collusion can be tacit or overt. Tacit collusion, such as setting similar prices, normally develops over time without any formal agreement. Overt collusion involves firms reaching an agreement that is unlikely to be publicised because such agreements are normally illegal, although certain cases are permitted in the UK. Collusion might result in the operation of a *cartel* or a *restrictive practice* such as exclusive supply.

communication: exchange of information or ideas between two or more parties.

■ Communication can take a number of forms, including oral, written and electronic. *Formal communication* takes place through official channels within a business, such as meetings or intranets. *Informal communication* takes place when unofficial channels are used to exchange information (e.g. gossip). Developments in information technology, particularly the Internet, have transformed communications within and between businesses.

■ *TIP* Communication is an important part of business studies and impinges on many aspects of business activity (e.g. marketing, industrial relations, motivation and leadership style).

communication channels: routes used to convey communications within an organisation.

■ *e.g.* the lines of command within the business from senior employee to subordinates (*vertical communication*) and between employees at the same level in the organisation, maybe at a team briefing (*horizontal communication*).

Companies Acts: series of Acts passed from 1844 to the present day governing the formation and operation of companies within the UK.

■ The Acts require companies to complete *Articles of Association* and *Memoranda of Association* when setting up, to divulge specific financial information and to operate their businesses within agreed guidelines. Many of the early Acts were consolidated in the Companies Act of 1985. A further Companies Act was passed in 1989 with the intention of bringing UK company legislation into line with that of the *European Union*.

company: general term for any incorporated business.

▨ Companies exist when a number of individuals contribute to a joint stock of *capital* in return for the ownership of *shares* in the business. Companies benefit from the privilege of *limited liability* and are legally separate from their owners (*shareholders*). In the UK, two main types of company exist. *Public limited companies* are larger, can sell their shares on the *Stock Exchange* and have the initials 'plc' after their name. *Private limited companies* are smaller, subject to less regulation and denoted by the term 'Ltd' after their name.

Competition Commission: a government organisation responsible for investigating proposed *mergers* and *takeovers* to check that they are in consumers' interests.

▨ The Competition Commission was known as the Monopolies and Mergers Commission (MMC) until 1999. It has two distinct functions. On its reporting side, the Commission has taken on the former MMC role of carrying out inquiries into monopolies, mergers and the regulation of privatised businesses. Second, the Commission hears appeals against decisions of the Director-General of Fair Trading concerning anti-competitive agreements and abuse by businesses of a dominant market position.

competition policy: series of rules and regulations operated by the UK and EU authorities with the intention of promoting free and fair competition within markets.

▨ Competition policy operates to avoid the exploitation of consumers through overcharging or the provision of unsatisfactory products. It covers the operation of *cartels* and *mergers* that might be against the public interest, the operation of *restrictive practices* intended to limit competition and the abuse by *monopolies* of their market power.

▨ *TIP* The *European Union* is becoming increasingly influential in shaping UK competition policy. If a conflict exists between UK and EU legislation on competition, the European laws take precedence.

computer-aided design: use of modern technology in the design stage of the production process.

▨ Businesses can produce accurate, three-dimensional drawings on computers which can be stored and easily updated as required. Designs can be tested and many faults eliminated before any manufacturing takes place. Computer-aided design is frequently used in conjunction with *computer-aided manufacture*.

▨ *e.g.* In 1999, Boeing, the aircraft manufacturer, designed and tested a new aeroplane on a computer, avoiding many of the teething problems associated with building a prototype. Firms in the clothing, packaging and motor vehicle industries also use computer-aided design extensively.

C

computer-aided manufacture: use of computers as an integral part of the production process.

■ Computers are used on *production lines* to manage the delivery of materials and components to the production line, and to control the operation of robots carrying out production activities. Using technology in this way offers businesses improvements in productivity and quality, although reorganisation and retraining of the workforce is normally essential. See also *computer-aided design*.

■ *e.g.* At its Luton factory, Vauxhall Motors uses computers to match production to orders as well as to operate robotic equipment.

conciliation: negotiation intended to reconcile differences between the parties to an industrial dispute.

■ A third party is usually at the heart of the attempt to bring the two parties together and to prolong the discussions, thereby lessening the possibility of industrial action. Conciliation is a 'softer' approach than *arbitration* as participation is not compulsory and the parties are not bound by the outcome of any investigation. The *Advisory, Conciliation and Arbitration Service* (ACAS) provides conciliation services to industry.

Confederation of British Industry (CBI): organisation representing the interests of British businesses on a wide range of issues.

■ The CBI was established in 1965 and represents the interests of over 3,500 companies. Its objective is to help create and sustain the conditions in which the UK can compete and prosper. Through its network of offices around the UK and in Brussels, the CBI represents its members' views on all business issues to the government and other national and international policy-makers. It supplies advice, information and research services to members on key public policy issues affecting business, and provides a forum for the exchange and encouragement of best management practice.

conglomerate: large business organisation having interests in a diverse range of industries.

■ Conglomerates are often created through a series of *mergers* and *takeovers* bringing together a varied grouping of organisations. The businesses that make up a conglomerate frequently have no direct relationship. Conglomerates supply a wide variety of goods and services, and trade in a variety of national and international markets. These factors make them less susceptible to sudden changes in the external environment.

■ *e.g.* Tomkins, a British conglomerate, has interests in food processing, gun manufacture (it owns Smith & Wesson) as well as bicycle manufacture and construction.

constructive dismissal: resignation of an employee when an employer behaves in a manner that demonstrates refusal to act within the terms of the individual's contract of employment.

■ In this situation, an employer behaves so unreasonably that it becomes intolerable for the employee to remain in his or her job. See also *unfair dismissal*.

▓ *e.g.* asking employees to undertake duties outside their contract of employment, such as working night shifts or working overseas for long periods.

consultation: process by which senior employees in an organisation discover the views of their subordinates.

▓ The information gathered in this way might influence decision making at a senior level within the organisation. Businesses use techniques such as *works councils* and worker directors to provide a means of consultation. *Trade unions* might also provide means by which senior managers can consult with employees at other levels in the organisation.

▓ *TIP* Consultation can be real or cosmetic. Some firms genuinely seek the views of their employees and take them into account when reaching important decisions. Others consult after a decision has been reached in an attempt to present a democratic image.

consumer: person or organisation that purchases products from a business for their own use, and not for resale.

▓ Consumers are influenced in purchasing decisions by a number of factors, including price, quality, after-sales service and customer service. Consumers generally have more influence in markets where firms are competing fiercely. Recently, a trend known as consumerism has resulted in consumers becoming more knowledgeable about goods and services. Organisations such as the Consumer's Association and its magazine *Which?* have contributed to an environment in which consumers are making more informed purchasing decisions.

consumer durable: product that purchasers use over a prolonged period.

▓ Consumer durables are generally expensive and are therefore infrequent purchases. They are often bought on *credit* by consumers and purchase decisions are sensitive to the government's *fiscal policy* and *monetary policy*, and especially to variations in *interest rates*. Firms supplying consumer durables often experience fluctuations in demand according to the stage of the *business cycle*. Consumer durables are in contrast to consumer non-durables, such as food, which are used over a short period of time.

▓ *e.g.* cars, televisions, audio equipment and mobile telephones.

consumer protection legislation: range of legislation designed to prevent *consumers* being subject to unfair or unscrupulous trading practices.

▓ Consumer protection legislation has developed steadily since the 1960s and provides consumers with assurance in relation to price, quality, safety and quantities.

▓ *e.g.* Key pieces of consumer protection legislation include the Trades Descriptions Act 1968, the Fair Trading Act 1973, the Consumer Credit Act 1974, the Sale of Goods Act 1979 and the Consumer Protection Act 1987.

contingency planning: process by which organisations attempt to forecast the future and to make preparations to deal with emergencies or crises that might occur.

■ A firm might have contingency plans to deal with a sudden slump in sales, the contamination of the production process or difficulties in acquiring essential resources. Firms only use contingency planning in preparation for events that are likely to happen, not for unexpected or unlikely happenings.

continuous improvement: see *kaizen*.

contribution: the difference between a product's *sales revenue* and its *variable costs*.

■ Contribution has two possible uses: to pay *fixed costs* and to provide *profits*. It is an important concept for firms that produce a number of products because it avoids the need to allocate fixed costs as in *absorption costing*.

■ *e.g.* In the following table, the contribution of the three products is £15,400,000. The firm has fixed costs of £8,000,000. From this information it is simple to calculate profits by deducting fixed costs from total contribution. Thus, in this case, profits are £7,400,000.

	Product A	Product B	Product C
Sales revenue (£000s)	12,750	18,500	24,000
Variable costs (£000s)	8,250	14,100	17,500
Contribution (£000s)	4,500	4,400	6,500
Fixed overheads = £8 million			

■ *TIP* Many students confuse contribution and profit, yet the distinction is vital. Profit is revenue less all costs, while contribution is revenue less variable costs only.

cooperative: organisation of persons who pool their resources to trade more efficiently than would be possible as individuals.

■ Members of cooperatives work together and share any profits generated. Cooperatives are found in manufacturing, marketing, wholesaling and banking as well as retailing. They differ from companies in that members only have a single vote, irrespective of the amount of money they invest, and that shares cannot be traded on the Stock Exchange. In spite of the recent success of the Co-operative Bank, cooperatives have not flourished in the UK due to difficulties in raising capital and attracting top-class management.

copyright: protection granted by the law to authors of written or recorded materials (e.g. books, films or music) for a specific period.

■ Copyright grants an author or composer the sole rights to benefit from his or her work for up to 70 years. Authors and composers can elect to sell their copyright to another person or organisation. Protection under copyright is granted automatically. Any infringement of copyright might result in a prosecution under *civil law*. Copyright on a work is indicated by the symbol ©. See also *patent* and *trade mark*.

corporate image: the public's perception of a business.

▓ Increasingly, businesses wish to present themselves as favourably as possible, recognising that they might gain a competitive advantage from being held in high esteem by *stakeholders*, and particularly customers. Many companies seek to improve their image by being adjudged to be socially responsible, showing concern for all groups with an interest in the business. This has led to the widespread publication of *social audits* and *environmental audits* to highlight the caring side of UK businesses.

▓ *e.g.* Nestlé, BP and Shell have spent heavily on corporate advertising to present their businesses in the best possible light.

corporate objectives: goals of the entire organisation.

▓ These *objectives* are based on the business's *mission statement* and vary according to the size and history of the business as well as the personal aims of senior managers. From its corporate objectives a business can set targets and goals at all levels in the organisation.

▓ *e.g.* survival, increasing market share, entering new markets (perhaps overseas), developing innovative goods and services, and earning the highest possible profits.

correlation: statistical technique used to establish the extent of the relationship between two variables.

▓ Correlation can be an important technique for those involved in *marketing*. For example, a business is likely to be interested to discover whether a close and positive relationship exists between the amount it spends on advertising and the level of sales achieved in the period immediately after. A positive correlation in these circumstances (meaning that spending on advertising and sales rise and fall together) is likely to encourage marketing managers to spend more on advertising.

cost: expenditure a business has to undertake in order to carry out its trading activities.

▓ Costs are charged against the income generated by a business and thus are an important determinant of the profits earned by a business. They can be categorised according to the area of the business incurring the expenditure (e.g. marketing, production or purchasing). A standard classification is to separate expenditure into *fixed costs* and *variable costs* according to whether they alter with the firm's level of output. Controlling and minimising costs is an important aspect of competing effectively.

cost centre: area, department or other part of a business for which expenditure can be calculated.

▓ It might be possible to ascertain the *costs* of operating an individual factory, producing a particular product, or running a specific retail outlet. Once this is achieved, it is possible to allocate *budgets* to minimise expenditure. The use of cost centres within a business not only assists in controlling costs, but also offers an opportunity to motivate staff by delegating financial authority for a given aspect of the business's operations.

■ **TIP** Students often confuse cost and *profit centres*. If it is possible to calculate the costs of a particular aspect of a business's activities, it is a cost centre. However, if costs and revenue (and hence profits) can be ascertained, the activity can be a profit centre. Thus a finance department is likely to be a cost centre, but a retail branch will probably be a profit centre.

cost-plus pricing: establishing the price of a product by calculating its cost of production and then adding an amount that is, in effect, profit.

■ By cost-plus pricing the manufacturer can be certain that the product will sell at a profit, but might be less sure about the level of sales. Cost-plus pricing does not take into account the state of the market or actions of competitors.

■ **e.g.** If a computer manufacturer is aware that a single product costs £500 to produce and decides to price the computer at £700, the pricing method is cost-plus.

counter-cyclical policy: series of economic policies implemented by the government with the intention of eliminating the worst effects of the *business cycle*.

■ The government can use *fiscal policy* and *monetary policy* to dampen the inflationary side-effects of a boom and to stimulate growth and spending during a slump. The intention is to promote stable growth in *gross national product*, as illustrated below.

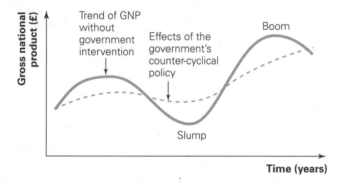

credit: financial arrangement under which an individual or a business is able to borrow money.

■ A business might borrow money from suppliers in the form of *trade credit*, or receive credit from the bank as an *overdraft* or a medium- or long-term loan. Credit offers advantages to businesses in that it is likely to improve their *cash flow*, and granting credit to customers by giving them time to settle their accounts can be an effective method of increasing sales. However, many forms of credit carry the penalty of interest charges. If credit is unauthorised (e.g. exceeding an agreed overdraft figure), the charges can be substantial.

creditors: individuals or businesses to which an organisation owes money.

■ Most businesses have creditors throughout their operations and this is a normal feature of trading. Creditors can take a number of forms. Suppliers of raw materials and components are creditors for a short period of time until their invoices are paid. Creditors are of value to a business since they offer interest-free loans. Creditors are recorded as a *current liability* on the *balance sheet*.

crisis management: series of techniques designed to help a business through a period of acute risk.

◼ In the event of a crisis occurring, a business should have a team prepared and trained to respond immediately. Businesses should ensure that internal and external communications are effective and that a decisive and consistent message is projected. Marketing is also an important tactic to counteract any adverse publicity. Even the largest companies might require crisis management.

◼ *e.g.* In 1999, the mighty Coca-Cola company suffered a series of crises, not least the discovery of contamination in bottles of its famous soft drink in several European countries.

critical path analysis: technique of analysing and organising the tasks to be carried out as part of a complex activity to determine the quickest and most efficient means of completing them.

◼ Critical path analysis avoids unnecessary delays and assists in keeping costs as low as possible. The tasks to be completed are shown in a network as a series of arrows linked to nodes that record information about starting and finishing times. Activities shown in parallel can be conducted at the same time. Each network contains a critical path, which is the sequence of activities that completes the project in the shortest possible time. The activities on this critical path cannot be delayed without delaying the entire project. Critical path analysis is often used for large-scale projects in construction and engineering to assist in making the most efficient use of expensive resources.

◼ *e.g.* The diagram shows a network for constructing and equipping a factory extension. This extension is to be completed as quickly as possible to minimise costs. The critical path is A–B–H.

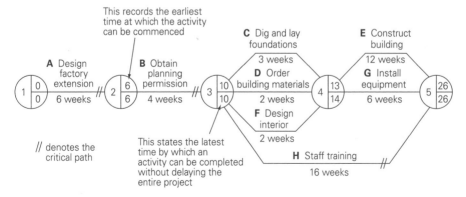

◼ *TIP* Do not simply focus on constructing critical path networks. It is also important to appreciate the advantages and disadvantages of this technique in any given circumstances.

culture: attitudes, ideas and beliefs that are shared by employees in a particular organisation.

■ The culture of an organisation is one of its most distinctive characteristics and one that develops over time. Business guru Charles *Handy* has identified a number of common types of business culture. Businesses with a traditional culture are bureaucratic and conventional. Businesses with a task culture focus on solving problems. A power culture places emphasis on charisma and risk taking. There is normally a strong relationship between culture and *organisational structure*.

current assets: items owned by a business that can readily be turned into *cash*.

■ Businesses need to hold sufficient assets to be able to meet short-term liabilities, but not so many as to tie up resources in an unprofitable form. See also *current liabilities*.

■ *e.g.* cash, money held at the bank, money owed by *debtors* and stocks of raw materials and finished goods.

current cost accounting: form of accounting in which a business takes account of *inflation* when constructing its financial statements.

■ This is a valuable approach during a period of rapidly rising prices and provides an accurate view of the profitability of a business.

current liabilities: short-term debts of an organisation, normally repaid within 1 year.

■ Businesses need to ensure that they hold sufficient assets to pay these short-term debts in order to avoid a *liquidity* crisis and losing the confidence of suppliers and investors. See also *current assets*.

■ *e.g.* a firm's *overdraft*, money owed to *creditors* and tax due.

current ratio: see *liquidity ratio*.

customer service: that aspect of a business's activities devoted to meeting customers' needs as fully as possible.

■ Some businesses operate a separate department to provide the highest possible standards of customer service. However, a more recent approach is to stress the role of each employee in satisfying consumers. In some industries (e.g. retailing and tourism), providing high standards of customer service is a means of gaining a competitive advantage.

customs duty: see *tariff*.

cyclical unemployment: *unemployment* associated with the *business cycle*.

■ Cyclical unemployment rises during a slump and declines in a boom.

■ *e.g.* Industries such as construction are particularly susceptible to this form of unemployment. During recessions and slumps, people are less likely to move home and demand new house building. At the same time, industry requires less building as order books are empty and *capacity* is under-utilised.

DCF: see *discounted cash flow*.

debenture: special type of long-term loan to be repaid at some future date, normally within 15 years of the loan being agreed.

■ The rate of interest paid on debentures is fixed. In some circumstances, debentures might not have a repayment date, representing a permanent loan to the business — this is an irredeemable debenture. Debentures are normally secured against the *assets* of the business. Debentures are *loan capital* and holders of debentures do not have voting rights at *annual general meetings*.

debtor: person or organisation owing money to businesses.

■ These debts might arise as a consequence of purchases for which customers have not yet paid, or because they have borrowed money from the business. All businesses have debtors as a normal part of their operations, and allowing customers time to pay can be an important part of breaking into a market or achieving growth. However, having too many debtors (or large amounts of money owed) can result in a business having *liquidity* problems and not being able to pay its own debts.

debtor days: the average time taken by a business's customers to pay for products bought on credit.

■ The formula used to measure debtor days is:

$$\text{debtor days} = \frac{\text{debtors}}{\text{sales revenue}} \times 365$$

A high figure (expressed in terms of days) indicates that customers are taking a long time to settle their debts. This might mean that the business suffers a shortage of *working capital*, requiring it to borrow money to purchase raw materials and pay wages. An effective credit control system can help to minimise the debtor days figure for any business.

■ *TIP* There is no established figure for debtor days — it depends upon the type of business. Supermarkets are paid immediately by their customers, so would expect a very low figure. House-builders might have a much higher figure.

decentralisation: passing authority from the centre of an organisation to those working elsewhere in the business.

■ Decentralisation might mean granting greater authority to employees in branches, departments or divisions of the business. It might also involve relocating jobs and functions (e.g. managing budgets) to other parts of the organisation. Many companies in the UK have decentralised their operations in the expectation of receiving a number of benefits. Decentralisation might result in quicker and more effective decisions taken by employees close to the customer. It might also result in more motivated employees who relish greater authority. However, it does rely upon good *communication* and a clear focus on organisational *objectives*.

■ *TIP* Students often confuse *delegation* and decentralisation. Delegation refers solely to passing authority down the organisational structure, while decentralisation primarily means passing authority out from the centre of the business to branches and divisions elsewhere.

decision tree: drawing representing the likely outcomes for a business of a number of courses of action and the financial consequences of each.

■ Decision trees are set out as shown below to record the costs and likely incomes from competing courses of action, using probability as a central part of the process. By calculating the expected incomes and costs, weighted to represent the probability of predictions proving correct, managers can select the course of action providing the highest expected income or profit.

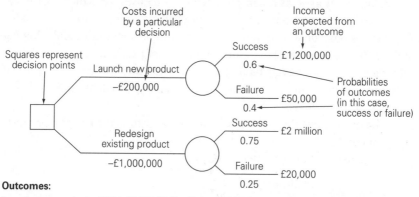

Outcomes:

Launch new product = (0.6 × £1,200,000) + (0.4 × £50,000) − £200,000 = £540,000

Redesign existing product = (0.75 × £2,000,000) + (0.25 × £20,000) − £1,000,000 = £505,000

Based on this, the company would launch a new product, as the expected income is higher.

Decision trees are a common technique used by businesses to reduce uncertainty as part of the decision-making process.

deed of partnership: document setting out the terms under which the two or more people forming a *partnership* agree to do business together.

■ The deed of partnership covers issues such as the amount of capital contributed by each of the partners to the business, shares of profits to be drawn by the partners and arrangements for decision making. All the partners must sign this document.

deflation: (1) situation in which the level of economic activity declines, characterised by falling levels of sales and production, and rising levels of unemployment.
▓ Governments normally take action to reverse declining levels of economic activity.
(2) situation when prices are falling over time — the opposite of *inflation*.
▓ *e.g.* This is a fairly unusual event, but it was commonplace in the 1930s.

delayering: reduction of *levels of hierarchy* within an *organisational structure*.
▓ Delayering has been a common tactic among UK businesses in recent years. Many organisations have removed middle managers as part of the process of delayering. It allows more authority to be granted to employees further down the structure, offering potential for improved motivation, while reducing wage costs.
▓ *e.g.* In 1999, following a policy of delayering, Barclays Bank made 6,000 employees redundant (about 10% of its workforce), many of whom were middle managers.

delegation: passing down authority to those lower in the organisational hierarchy.
▓ Delegation offers employees the chance to take more control over their working lives on a day-to-day basis and is expected to improve the performance of the workforce. Delegation often accompanies *democratic leadership* and can provide relatively junior employees with greater satisfaction from their work.
▓ *TIP* It is important not to confuse authority and responsibility. Remember that a manager can delegate authority to complete a particular task, but cannot pass down responsibility — this always remains with the senior employee.

demand: amount of some good or service that consumers wish to purchase at a given price over a specified period.
▓ Many businesses forecast future demand as a means of calculating their expected future income (level of demand multiplied by likely selling price). Demand for a firm's product can be affected by a number of factors, including the income levels of consumers, the actions of rival firms (e.g. launching new products or engaging in advertising campaigns) and the price charged. The relationship between price charged for a product and the level of demand for it is explained by the theory of *price elasticity of demand*.

demerger: uncoupling two or more businesses.
▓ Demerger might take place because the market has changed or because the business as a single entity is deemed not to have been a success. Demergers have become more common over recent years. See also *merger*.
▓ *e.g.* In 2000, P&O demerged its cruise liner business from the remainder of its activities, notably operating ferries between the UK and the Continent.

democratic leadership (also called 'participative leadership'): style of *leadership* in which the majority within the organisation agree decisions.
▓ Democratic leadership relies upon employees, particularly senior managers,

possessing good communication skills and encouraging *two-way communication*. This leadership style encourages participation by employees and can make considerable use of *delegation*. It can be particularly effective when complex decisions have to be made, requiring a range of specialist skills. This style of leadership can motivate employees, but it might result in slow decision-making.

■ *TIP* Students often argue that this style of leadership is 'best'. This may or may not be true depending upon circumstances. Democratic leadership might be inappropriate if quick decisions are needed or if the workforce is unskilled.

demutualisation: conversion of building societies, insurance companies and other *mutual organisations* into *public limited companies*.

■ Many famous mutual organisations have become companies, and members of these organisations have been offered large financial inducements to persuade them to vote for change. However, the decision of Standard Life's members not to demutualise may indicate that the trend is slowing.

■ *e.g.* There have been many examples of demutualisation in the UK over recent years, as former building societies (for example, the Halifax and Northern Rock) have become banks operating as plcs with their shares quoted on the Stock Exchange. Demutualisation has also extended to friendly societies providing insurance services — the Scottish Widows Group has been taken over by the Lloyds TSB bank group as a result of its demutualisation.

■ *TIP* Do not assume that demutualisation must be a good move. The performance of the newly created banks has not always been as good as that of the remaining mutual building societies. The trend for demutualisation might be slowing, as shown by the decision of the members of Standard Life to vote against the change.

depreciation: loss in value of a business's *assets* over a period of time.

■ Depreciation in effect allocates the cost of a *fixed asset* such as machinery or vehicles over the lifetime of the asset in question. This gives the managers and owners of businesses a truer indication of the actual cost of operating the business than does including the entire costs of an asset at the time it is purchased. A figure for depreciation is normally included in the *profit and loss account*, reducing profits and the business's liability to pay tax.

■ *TIP* Depreciation causes some confusion among students of business studies. It is only an allowance made by businesses in recognition that the cost of purchasing major assets should be spread over the useful life of the asset. It is not a system of saving, whereby businesses prepare to replace an expensive asset.

deregulation: reduction of the degree of government control over an aspect of business activity.

■ Particular markets in the UK have been deregulated in recent years, allowing freer and fairer competition between competing firms.

■ *e.g.* BT previously had a monopoly in the provision of telecommunication services within the UK. Other firms were allowed to enter the market in the expectation that consumers would benefit from this move through lower prices and improved quality of service.

desk research: form of *market research* in which businesses use data collected previously for other purposes.

A firm might use government documents or the results of research carried out by other organisations. This offers the benefit of being readily available and cheap to collect and use. However, the data might be out of date or not entirely relevant to the purposes of the research. See also *field research*.

destroyer pricing: see *predatory pricing*.

devaluation: when a country's currency loses value against the currencies of other nations as a result of a decision by the government.

Devaluation takes place within a *fixed exchange rate* system, whereby rates are not determined by market forces. Fixed systems of exchange rates are rare today, with most currencies finding their value on world markets as a result of normal trading activities. Many businesses benefit from a devaluation of the currency, as their exports become cheaper overseas, while imports of foreign goods and services are likely to become more expensive.

direct cost: expenditure that can be clearly allocated to a particular product or aspect of production.

The cost of purchasing raw materials might be easily allocated to the production of a particular product. This might be important is assessing profitability within a multi-product firm. It is normal for direct costs to vary proportionately with the level of a firm's output.

direct mail: material distributed through the postal system to the homes and businesses of existing and potential customers.

Direct mail is often referred to as 'junk mail'. Most direct mail is sent to people and organisations on mailing lists, which are sometimes purchased from other organisations. It is used extensively by the financial services sector in the UK.

e.g. Direct mail can range from a simple letter introducing or promoting a product to catalogues or even product samples.

TIP It should be considered in conjunction with *market segmentation*, as it is a means of targeting marketing at the most relevant elements of the market.

director: person appointed by the *shareholders* of a company to participate in the management of the organisation.

Directors are elected at the company's *annual general meeting* and are granted powers to play a central part in the running of the business. The directors of a business work together as a *board of directors* to determine and oversee the company's strategy. Directors might be executive directors, in which case they are full-time employees responsible for key functions such as finance or marketing. Other directors are non-executive, employed on a part-time basis for some special skill or knowledge they might bring to board meetings.

direct response marketing: any form of *promotion* that encourages current and potential consumers to contact the firm directly.

■ This might simply be through the completion of a form, telephoning a free-phone number or responding by e-mail to a business's website. Consumers might contact the business to request further information on its products. The intention is to develop a direct relationship with customers, to build up clear profiles of potential customers as well as compiling an up-to-date mailing list. It also allows businesses to assess the effectiveness of various forms of marketing in attracting the attention of customers.

■ *TIP* This is becoming an increasingly important form of marketing and has led to many businesses developing direct selling, whereby they supply goods and services directly to the customer.

discounted cash flow (DCF): expresses the worth of some future cash flow in terms of its present-day value.

■ This is an important technique used in *investment appraisal* to allow the effective comparison of alternative investment projects. The technique of discounted cash is based on the premise that money received soon is worth more than an equivalent amount received at some time in the future. Indeed, the longer the delay before any inflow, the less its present-day value. By using an agreed interest rate as part of the calculation of discounted cash flow, it is possible to compare projects with different patterns of income and expenditure.

diseconomies of scale: financial disadvantages that can result from the growth of a business.

■ Diseconomies are usually associated with the bureaucracy and disorganisation that frequently result from increasing the scale of operations. Managing a large organisation is complex, and inefficiencies might result from lack of communication and insufficient coordination. These can cause increasing costs of production. See also *economies of scale*.

disposable income: income or earnings available to a consumer after deducting income tax and national insurance.

■ This represents the income that is available to the consumer to spend or save. Disposable income can be important data for businesses (especially those selling luxury goods), as it provides some indication of likely levels of demand.

■ *TIP* Confusion often occurs between disposable income and discretionary income. The latter relates to a consumer's income after essential expenditure, such as that on accommodation.

distribution (also called 'place'): range of activities necessary to make goods and services available to a customer once production is complete.

■ Distribution might entail the use of some intermediaries, such as wholesalers and retailers, and involves important activities such as *packaging*, transportation and display. Distribution is an important element of the *marketing mix*.

distribution channels: routes used by companies to get their goods and services to customers.

■ Shorter channels of distribution are becoming favoured as firms opt to supply customers directly to increase their control over the market and their profits.

Such channels might take a number of forms, as shown below.

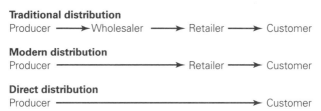

Traditional distribution
Producer ⟶ Wholesaler ⟶ Retailer ⟶ Customer

Modern distribution
Producer ⟶ Retailer ⟶ Customer

Direct distribution
Producer ⟶ Customer

- *e.g.* The UK insurance market has changed dramatically in recent years, with companies such as Norwich Union Direct dealing with customers without using the service of insurance brokers as intermediaries.

diversification: approach whereby businesses produce an increased range of unrelated goods and services.

- Diversification is often intended to spread risk. If one product becomes obsolete or goes out of fashion, having other, very different products will provide an income for the business while it develops replacement products. It avoids having 'all one's eggs in one basket' and is the principle behind the creation of *conglomerates*.

divestment: removal of a *subsidiary* part of a business, through its sale or closure.

- The subsidiary could be a separate company or a department or division of the main business. Divestment might be the result of a decision by the *Competition Commission* because a business has an unfair competitive advantage, or it might happen because a particular element of a business is no longer required or is unprofitable.

- *e.g.* In 2000, Vodafone, the mobile phone company, was forced to sell its rival Orange. Vodafone had taken over the German company Mannesmann which owned Orange.

dividends: that part of a company's profits paid to its *shareholders*.

- Dividends are payment made in return for shareholders making their funds available to the company. They can be fixed or variable according to the type of *share*, and decisions about the amount of dividends to be paid are taken by the *board of directors* and discussed at the *annual general meeting*.

dividend yield: ratio showing the return received by a company's *shareholders* as a percentage of the *market price* of the firm's *shares*.

- The formula used to calculate dividend yield is:

$$\text{dividend yield} = \frac{\text{dividend per share}}{\text{market price of share}} \times 100$$

A higher figure is more satisfactory for shareholders who are seeking an immediate return on their investment in the form of *dividends*. A lower figure than that achieved by other companies might indicate an unprofitable business or one that is retaining a high proportion of its profits for reinvestment.

divorce of ownership from control: situation in which the people who own a business do not actually control it.

■ This is commonplace in companies and especially in large *public limited companies. Shareholders* can exercise control at *annual general meetings,* but many do not attend and few have any real understanding of business matters. Thus the *directors* have almost complete control.

■ *e.g.* Firms such as BT and Shell have many thousands of shareholders who own the company, but control is effectively in the hands of the business's directors.

downtime: period when machinery or other equipment within a business is idle as a result of breakdowns, or adjustments being required.

■ Firms seek to minimise the amount of time that their equipment is unproductive, as they are incurring costs (e.g. hire of the equipment) without generating any income. Modern businesses aim to switch machinery from one use to another with a minimum of downtime.

duopoly: situation in which a market comprises two producers only.

■ Traditionally, a duopoly is regarded as being against the interests of consumers, since the lack of competition might result in high prices and insufficient product innovation. See also *monopoly.*

■ *e.g.* Microsoft and Intel operate a duopoly as the only two significant producers of personal computer technology.

■ *TIP* The above example illustrates the problems that duopolies might encounter. The US authorities have taken action against the Microsoft–Intel duopoly on the grounds that it prevents free and fair competition.

earliest start time (EST): measurement used in *critical path analysis* to indicate the first date at which a particular activity can commence.

■ This timing takes into account the time required for previous activities. It is important for managers to know the EST of an activity to ensure that resources are available at the right time and do not lie idle. The EST on the final activity of a network shows the earliest date at which the entire project can be completed. See also *latest finish time*.

earnings: income or revenue received by an individual or organisation.

■ Businesses receive earnings in a variety of forms, including revenue from selling goods and services, rent from the lease of property and other assets, and interest from investments in other organisations. See also *income*.

Easdaq: stock exchange dealing in *shares* from companies throughout Europe.

■ Since its establishment in 1996, Easdaq has been the only stock market operating on a truly pan-European basis, allowing investors and businesses to trade across European borders without difficulty. The exchange uses technology to provide information about the share prices of listed companies. Most companies whose shares are quoted on Easdaq are in the telecommunications, information technology, software and biotechnology sectors.

■ *TIP* Easdaq is a high-technology market allowing the purchase and sale of companies' shares on an international basis. Other high-technology stock exchanges exist, such as Nasdaq in the USA. Mergers and/or takeovers are likely in this sector.

e-commerce (also called 'electronic commerce' and 'on-line trading')**:** use of computers and electronic communications in business transactions.

■ E-commerce might include the use of electronic data interchange (EDI), electronic money exchange, Internet advertising, Web sites and on-line databases. Increasing numbers of companies are now engaging in e-commerce: for example, the major UK banks all offer their financial services via the *Internet*. However, few businesses have discovered how to make this a profitable form of business.

■ *e.g.* Two well-known Internet businesses are Amazon (an on-line bookshop) and Smile (a bank).

economic growth: increase in the value of goods and services produced by a nation's economy.

■ Economic growth is normally measured by an increase in *gross national product*. Most countries' economies experience economic growth over a period of time, although in the short term economies might stagnate or even decline in size. A period of economic growth is associated with the upswing stage of the *business cycle* and offers businesses the benefits expected from a period of prosperity: increasing sales and rising revenues and, possibly, profits. However, periods of fast economic growth are not sustainable and often result in *inflation*.

■ *TIP* It is easy to discuss the benefits of economic growth, but a well-balanced argument would recognise that it has disadvantages too. Pollution is more likely, prices might rise and an economic *slump* might occur as a consequence of economic growth, particularly if the government does not manage it effectively.

economic order quantity (EOQ): optimal amount of materials or goods that can be ordered to minimise costs.

■ By calculating an EOQ, a firm can incur the lowest possible expenses in terms of ordering and storing raw materials and other stocks, while being able to meet the demands of its customers. Factors affecting this calculation include storage costs, costs associated with loss through perishing or obsolescence, as well as the costs of placing an order and transporting the items.

■ *e.g.* The formula to calculate an economic order quantity is:

$$EOQ = \sqrt{\frac{2 \times U \times OC}{UC \times SC}}$$

where *U* is the annual usage of the item in number of units, *OC* is the cost of placing a single order, *UC* is the unit cost of the stock, and *SC* is the storage cost per annum.

economies of scale: decline in the cost of producing a single unit of production as a consequence of increasing the size of the firm's operations.

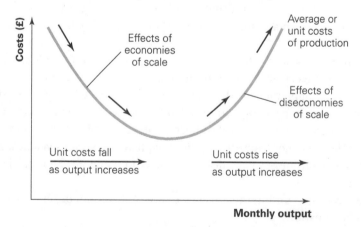

■ The decline in unit costs might result from purchasing economies, possibly through bulk-buying raw materials and components. Firms might also experience technical economies of scale through using more efficient machinery. This might be employed most effectively when producing large quantities of output. These are all examples of internal economies of scale that relate to a single firm within an industry. All the firms in an industry benefit from external economies of scale. These might result from improved transport links to a particular locality or training for the labour force, perhaps paid for by the government. See also *diseconomies of scale* and *unit cost*.

EDI: see *electronic data interchange*.

efficiency: relationship between the inputs to a production process and its output.

■ Efficiency is said to increase if a firm can produce a greater output with fewer inputs or resources. Efficiency also improves if output can be maintained with fewer resources being used in production. The concept of efficiency can be used to measure the contribution of particular types of resources used in production, such as *labour* or *capital*. Firms might gain a competitive advantage from improving efficiency because this results in reduced costs of production. A more efficient firm is therefore able to sell at lower prices or enjoy increased profits. Efficiency is an important theme in business studies. See also *productivity*.

electronic commerce: see *e-commerce*.

electronic data interchange (EDI): conversion of a transmitted document into a format readable by the receiving computer.

e-mail: a system that sends messages on computers via local or global networks.

■ As opposed to traditional mail services, e-mail sends messages instantaneously anywhere in the world. It possesses the capability to send messages at any time, to anyone with access to the *Internet*, for less money than it would cost to mail a letter or to make a telephone call. Linked by high-speed data connections that create a global network, e-mail allows individuals and businesses to compose messages and transmit them in seconds to one or more recipients across the office, the street or the country. Use of e-mail is expanding rapidly, threatening businesses that supply more traditional forms of communication, such as postal services.

employment protection legislation: series of Acts of Parliament intended to ensure that employees are treated fairly in the workplace.

■ These Acts relate to a range of issues, including contracts of employment, *health and safety*, industrial relations and *trade union* activity. Some legislation relates to individuals, such as the Race Relations Act and the Sex Discrimination Act, which prevent discrimination on the grounds of race or sex. Other employment protection legislation is collective in effect and relates to the activities of trade unions and the process of *collective bargaining*. A series of Employment Acts in the 1980s restricted the powers of trade unions.

empowerment: granting employees greater control over their working lives.

▨ Empowerment entails giving employees greater authority to organise their own work, and to take decisions without reference to managers. It potentially offers businesses the benefit of more motivated employees, improved *productivity* and lower *labour turnover*. However, it is likely to require significant *training* if employees are to be able to fulfil the employer's expectations.

EMU: see *European Monetary Union.*

end user: see *ultimate consumer.*

enterprise zones: small inner-city areas in which businesses receive high levels of government support to encourage business investment.

▨ Enterprise zones were introduced in the budget of 1981 with the intention of attracting firms to the inner cities. The aim was to promote prosperity in these depressed areas and to offer increased employment opportunities. Firms moving into enterprise zones and creating jobs were offered the factories rent-free for a period of time, rebates on business rates and grants towards capital expenditure.

▨ *e.g.* Enterprise zones were created in most UK cities, including Belfast, London, Newcastle, Cardiff and Birmingham.

entrepreneur: person establishing or operating a business and thereby taking a financial risk.

▨ Entrepreneurs seek new business opportunities, invest in them and hope to generate profits. Many entrepreneurs fail, but the rewards for success can be enormous.

▨ *e.g.* Richard Branson (Virgin) and Bill Gates (Microsoft) have amassed fortunes by creating hugely successful businesses.

environmental audit (also called 'green audit')**:** independent assessment of the effects of a business's activities upon the environment.

▨ For many businesses, environmental audits are a *public relations* exercise intended to reassure customers that the firm is not guilty of damaging the environment. They can be a means of gaining competitive advantage by improving the public's perception of businesses.

▨ *e.g.* Firms with considerable potential to pollute (for example, oil companies such as Shell and BP) have been among the early adopters of environmental audits.

EOQ: see *economic order quantity.*

equity capital: that part of a company's funds owned by its *shareholders.*

▨ Equity capital might comprise the money originally subscribed by shareholders when purchasing shares as well as any *reserves* and *profit* reinvested in the business. Equity capital is an important *source of finance*, and one on which a fixed payment is not due. Holders of equity capital receive returns in the form of *dividends*, which vary according to the profitability of the company.

equity share: see *ordinary share.*

EST: see *earliest start time.*

ethics: moral attitudes and principles held by individuals and organisations.

■ A business that takes decisions that are morally correct, as opposed to most profitable, might be considered to be ethical. Thus, a business might opt to use a resource that is from a sustainable source, even if it is more expensive. In this way, it is placing principles ahead of profits. Ethics have attracted a great deal of attention over the last 20 years and an increasing number of businesses have adopted ethical policies throughout their organisations.

■ *e.g.* The Co-operative Bank has used its ethical stance as a successful strategy to differentiate its services from those offered by other banks.

■ *TIP* Remember that adopting an ethical stance can pose problems for businesses as well as providing advantages. It might be most useful to businesses whose products are very similar to those supplied by rivals.

EU: see *European Union*.

European Central Bank: a bank, based in Frankfurt in Germany, that has responsibility for the conduct of *monetary policy* in the 11 countries that have adopted the European single currency (the euro).

■ The Bank, founded in 1998, works alongside national central banks (such as Germany's Bundesbank) to set interest rates in all countries using the euro. It will also be the sole issuer of euro notes and coins. It is charged with the duty of overseeing the implementation of *European Monetary Union* (EMU). At the time of writing, Britain had not joined the euro and had no say in the running of the Bank. The Bank replaced the European Monetary Institute.

European Commission: organisation responsible for proposing new policies and legislation for the *European Union*.

■ The Commission also has responsibility for carrying out decisions taken by the European Union's decision-making body, the Council of Ministers. The Commission is based in Brussels and comprises 20 commissioners (appointed by member states) supported by a large clerical staff.

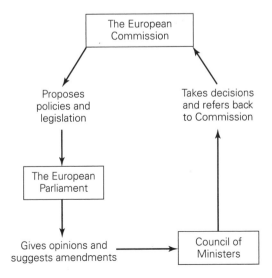

European Monetary Union (EMU): the bringing together of the monetary and financial systems of participating states and the introduction of a single currency.

■ In 1998, the *European Central Bank* was formed to plan and operate a uniform *monetary poli*cy. EMU saw the introduction of a common European currency (the euro) in January 1999, following a period during which the values of a number of European currencies were tied together. From 1999, 11 European states participated in EMU using the new currency for payment between banks. Some countries (e.g. France) have priced their goods and services in euros as well as their national currency. Notes and coins for the euro will be available from 2002. Four members of the *European Union* (including the UK) have not taken full membership of EMU and have no immediate plans to adopt the euro.

■ *TIP* This is a potentially confusing area. The European Monetary System (EMS) was the predecessor of EMU and entailed tying together European currencies to avoid wide fluctuations in *exchange rates*. This was an important step in the creation of a single currency.

European Union (EU): organisation of 15 European countries aiming to operate common economic, social and foreign policies.

■ The European Union was established under the Treaty of Maastricht in 1992 and replaced the European Community. The establishment of the European Union is part of a process of bringing together many European countries. It began with the Treaty of Rome in 1958. Initially, European unification offered free trade and a degree of coordination between separate economies. The creation of the European Union brought together the economies of the member states by removing barriers to trade and creating a unified *monetary policy* and a single currency — the euro. In spite of the initial refusal of four states (including the UK) to adopt the single currency, the establishment of the European Union is seen by some as a step along the road towards political union — a United States of Europe. See also *European Monetary Union*.

excess capacity (also called 'overcapacity' and 'under-utilised capacity'): where a business or an industry is not using its productive resources to their full potential.

■ In these circumstances, a business might have unused labour, factory space or equipment. These resources might not be used at all or might only be utilised for part of the working week. Excess capacity poses a major problem for businesses if it continues in the long term. Businesses incur costs for resources that are not generating income, resulting in higher prices and/or lower profitability. This can affect competitiveness and might be remedied by selling surplus *fixed assets, redundancy* or seeking new markets.

exchange rate: price of one currency expressed in terms of another.

e

■ Most currencies are traded on the world's foreign exchange markets and their exchange rates alter daily. For many years until 1971, *fixed exchange rates* existed whereby the values of currencies remained unchanged for long periods of time. Since then most currencies have 'floated', meaning that they are usually left to find their own value on the foreign exchange markets, although occasionally governments have attempted to intervene to influence their value. One exception to allowing currencies to float was the European Monetary System, under which a number of European currencies were locked together in the 1980s and 1990s.

■ *e.g.* At the time of writing, the exchange rate of the pound was 9.85 French francs, 350 Greek drachmas or 1.55 American dollars.

■ *TIP* Questions requiring knowledge of exchange rates are common. However, it is important to remember that, although a change in an exchange rate affects the price of exports and imports, this does not mean that demand will vary. The effect of a change in the value of a currency on demand for exports, for example, will depend upon the *price elasticity of demand* for the products concerned.

expectancy theory: theory based upon the principle that people are motivated by the expected outcomes of their actions.

■ Expectancy theories contend that employees can be motivated to behave in certain ways through the expectation that the outcome will be desirable to them. This theory of *motivation* is associated with the work of Victor Vroom and is in contrast to theories, such as Abraham *Maslow*'s, which relate motivation to human needs.

extension strategy: series of techniques used to extend the period of time over which a product achieves high levels of sales.

■ The term is used in connection with the *product life cycle* and describes how businesses extend the maturity stage of the cycle, postponing the inevitable onset of the decline stage. Extension strategies might include revamping (but not radically altering) a product or aiming it at new markets or segments.

■ *e.g.* Imperial Tobacco, recognising that sales of cigarettes have declined in Europe and North America, switched its attention to China — a market with nearly one billion potential smokers and little health education.

external financing: raising funds from sources outside the business.

■ Major methods of external finance are *loan capital* and *share capital*. External finance is particularly vital to newly established firms or those that are growing rapidly. Loans might be short term (perhaps in the form of an *overdraft*) to help overcome cash-flow difficulties, or long term (perhaps in the form of *mortgages* or *debentures*) to purchase fixed assets. Share issues can raise large sums for investment, but might result in the owners losing control of a business.

extrapolation: analyses the past performance of a variable such as sales and extends this into the future.

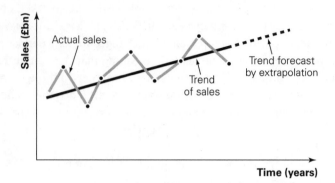

If a firm has enjoyed a steady increase in sales over a number of years, extrapolation is likely to forecast a continued steady rise. Extrapolation is easy to carry out as it merely involves extending a *trend*, but it might be inaccurate because it assumes that the future will be similar to the past. For this reason, it is not suitable for use in environments subject to rapid change.

factoring: selling customer accounts before they are due for less than their face value.

■ A firm might have an outstanding account on which a customer owes, say, £100,000 due in 2 months' time. It is possible, by factoring, to sell this debt for an immediate payment of approximately 80% of its value (£80,000 in our example) and a further 15% or thereabouts (£15,000) once the organisation offering the factoring service receives payment. A business using factoring receives an immediate injection of cash, but loses about 5% of its revenue. Factoring can be used in relation to overseas and domestic customer accounts.

■ *TIP* Factoring is one of several techniques that businesses might use to improve their *cash flow*. However, it is not suitable for firms with small profit margins, as the charges might exceed the profits they expect from the account.

factors of production: the four elements — land, labour, capital and enterprise — used in the production of goods and services.

■ Land as a factor of production is assumed to include all natural resources (e.g. mineral deposits). Labour covers all human inputs to the production process, whether physical or mental. Capital encompasses all man-made resources used in production. Enterprise is the bringing together of the other resources — a risk normally taken in pursuit of profit.

Fair Trading Act: an Act of 1973 that consolidated previous legislation relating to the control of *monopolies* and *mergers*, and extended its scope.

■ The Act created the *Office of Fair Trading* (and the role of the Director-General of Fair Trading) to implement and coordinate all aspects of controlling monopolies and mergers and restrictive practices. The Act also gave the Office of Fair Trading responsibility for referring monopoly and merger situations for investigation by the Monopolies and Mergers Commission (now the *Competition Commission*). In addition, the Act gave the Office of Fair Trading powers to oversee the design and operation of consumer protection legislation in the UK.

feedback: the response stage within *communication*.

■ Feedback confirms the receipt of communication as well as providing an exchange of ideas.

■ *e.g.* replies to letters, faxes or e-mails; comments or criticisms on a business's presentations or advertising campaigns.

■ *TIP* Feedback is one of the indicators that high-quality communication is taking place within an organisation. It is also an indicator of *democratic leadership* that encourages two-way communication.

field research: gathering information through direct contact with potential customers, using methods such as interviews, *questionnaires* and observation.

■ Field research is costly and can take time to conduct and analyse, but it has the potential to provide high-quality data on which managers might base their marketing decisions. Field research is more likely to be used by firms trading in markets where consumers' tastes and fashions change regularly. See also *market research* and *desk research*.

FIFO: see *first in, first out*.

financial year: see *year (financial)*.

first in, first out (FIFO): system of valuing stocks of raw materials and finished goods in which items that are bought earliest are judged to be used first during an *accounting period*.

■ In some businesses (e.g. supermarkets), stock is actually handled in this way to avoid items perishing. In manufacturing industries, where stock could be non-perishable, stock might be used more randomly. However, for accounting purposes it is common to assume that stocks are used in this way. In a period of inflation, the FIFO system of *stock valuation* tends to show lower costs and higher profits, raising the tax liability of the business.

■ *TIP* The Inland Revenue only accepts certain methods of stock valuation: it approves FIFO, but not the *last in, first out* method, in spite of its benefits to businesses in periods of inflation.

fiscal policy: government's use of *taxation* and *public spending* to manage the economy.

■ Governments can use fiscal policy to alleviate the worst fluctuations of the *business cycle* and so control unemployment and inflation. By cutting taxation and/or raising its own expenditure, the government can stimulate the level of activity in the economy, raising production and consumers' expenditure. Conversely, the government can dampen the level of activity by raising taxation rates or reducing public expenditure.

■ *TIP* Recent UK governments have not made extensive use of fiscal policy to manage the economy, preferring to rely upon *monetary policy*. It is important to show examiners that your understanding of this area of business studies is not entirely theoretical.

fiscal year: see *year (fiscal)*.

fixed assets: items owned by a business that it expects to retain for 1 year or more.

■ Fixed assets are not bought for resale. They are recorded (along with other types of *asset*) on a business's *balance sheet*. Manufacturing firms (e.g. car manufacturers such as Ford) need to purchase large amounts of fixed assets to engage in production. The value of fixed assets on the balance sheet is normally reduced over time (with the possible exceptions of land and property) through the process of *depreciation*. Businesses providing services (e.g. accountants and doctors) might not need to invest so heavily.

■ *e.g.* land, property, machinery and vehicles.

fixed costs: expenses that do not change (at least in the short term) when a firm alters its level of output. See also *variable costs*.

■ *e.g. depreciation*, rent and rates.

fixed exchange rates: system where a nation's currency is maintained at a stable value in relation to other currencies as a result of government *intervention* in foreign exchange markets.

■ The authorities buy and sell their own currency with the aim of maintaining its exchange value against other currencies. However, if a currency is thought to be overvalued, a government might not have large enough reserves of foreign currency to be able to purchase sufficient amounts of its own currency. Fixed exchange rates can provide firms trading internationally with a stable environment in which to do business. Maintaining fixed exchange rates was commonplace until 1971, and even in the 1980s the UK was attempting to maintain the value of the pound against European currencies.

flexible specialisation: when a firm has organised its production so as to be able to respond to patterns of demand that might change regularly.

■ Flexible firms are able to produce batches of products that exactly meet the requirements of customers, ensuring high levels of satisfaction. Manufacturing in this way requires highly skilled and adaptable employees as well as multi-purpose technology. Successful flexible specialisation might give a firm an important competitive advantage.

flexible working: when a labour force is organised so as to be able to respond to the changing demands of the organisation.

■ Flexible working might require employees to be multi-skilled and able to carry out a variety of tasks, to work part-time and to be available for short-term contracts. With a flexible workforce, a business is able to cope with sudden changes in demand or fashion and to cover for absent employees without disruption. Flexible working includes teleworking and flexible hours (where employees work variable hours each week, subject to an annual maximum).

flotation: making the *shares* in a company available on the *Stock Exchange* for the first time.

■ A flotation might result from the decision of a *private limited company* to convert to a *public limited company*. A flotation normally involves a company producing a prospectus to promote its value as an investment and to invite the purchase of shares.

■ *e.g.* The Internet-based business, Lastminute.com, was floated in this way in 2000.

flow production: see *mass production*.

formal communication: exchange of information and ideas within and outside a business using official channels.

■ Formal communication might take place at board meetings or team briefings, through e-mail, memos and letters as well as through advertising. Effective formal communication is a crucial element in successful management. See also *communication* and *informal communication*.

franchise: the granting by one business (the franchisor) to another individual or business the rights to supply its products.

■ The company purchasing the rights to supply products (the franchisee) will normally be expected to pay an initial fee and then a percentage of profits or sales revenue for the period of the franchise. In return, the franchisor will give permission for the franchisee to use the business's name and image and to supply the goods or services, often within an agreed area. Franchisees might also benefit from training and national advertising. Franchises are popular as they offer *entrepreneurs* a ready-made business and some of the benefits of large-scale production.

■ *e.g.* McDonald's and Burger King operate many of their restaurants as franchises.

■ *TIP* Some students are under the misapprehension that a franchise is another legal form of a business. Franchises can take a number of legal forms, including *sole traders, partnerships* and *private limited companies*.

free enterprise: philosophy that supports the view that business should be allowed to trade with minimal interference from the government.

■ Free enterprise encourages a minimal use of legislation to control business activity, relying upon competition to curb undesirable behaviour. Governments and businesses have argued that production is more efficient and living standards higher under free enterprise. This is a view supported by increasing numbers of governments across the world, particularly since the decline of the communist regimes in eastern Europe. The extensive *privatisation* of many former government-run industries is evidence of the growing acceptance of the free enterprise philosophy.

frictional unemployment: *unemployment* that arises from people changing their jobs.

■ Many employees do not move immediately from one job to another, but spend a limited amount of time out of work. This type of unemployment is normal in a healthy economy, but it can be reduced through the efficient provision of information on job vacancies.

fringe benefits: payments made to employees other than *wages* or *salaries*.

■ Some fringe benefits, notably *share options,* can be very attractive to employees and are often an indication of an employee's status within the organisation.

■ *e.g.* company cars, share options, non-contributory pensions and private health insurance.

full costing: method of costing under which all costs (direct and indirect) are allocated to a *cost centre* within a business.

By allocating all costs in this way, a business can assess the total costs of some aspect of its activities and ensure that it sets prices so as to earn a profit. It is sometimes difficult to allocate *indirect costs* fairly, which can result in obtaining inaccurate figures from this type of costing. See also *absorption costing*.

gearing: measures the ratio between a company's *share capital* and its long-term borrowing.

■ A company will normally aim to raise a maximum of 50% of its *capital* through borrowing. If gearing exceeds 50%, a company is described as *overgeared* and is vulnerable to rises in *interest rates*. Shareholders are likely to find highly geared companies an unattractive investment because once the company has met the fixed interest charges on its borrowing, the amount remaining to be paid as dividends might be low.

■ *TIP* There are two methods of measuring gearing. One compares the amount of capital raised through borrowing with the amount raised by the sale of shares. The second compares the amount of capital raised through borrowing with the company's entire capital. When analysing a gearing figure, it is important to recognise which form of the ratio has been used.

general union: association of workers that do not have a single common skill and do not work in the same industry.

■ Such unions represent workers in a range of industries and tend to have large numbers of members. General unions have become more common in the UK as a result of a series of mergers between smaller, more specialist unions.

■ *e.g.* One of the UK's largest unions is the Transport and General Workers' Union with approximately 900,000 members who work in every region of Great Britain and Ireland and in every industrial sector.

globalisation: the trend for many markets to become worldwide in scope.

■ Improvements in transport and communications (notably the Internet) have encouraged the development of global markets. Because of globalisation, many businesses now trade throughout the world, whereas in the past they might have focused on one country or region, such as Europe. Supporters of globalisation point out benefits in terms of a wider choice of products and lower prices. Opponents believe that it will result in uniform products worldwide and the loss of cultural diversity.

GNP: see *gross national product*.

goodwill: *intangible asset* arising from a business's good reputation, established brand names and existing customer contracts.

g

▓ Goodwill is measured by the difference between the market value of a business and its net assets as recorded on its balance sheet. See also *amortisation*.

▓ *e.g.* An engineering firm might be sold to a larger business for £4 million, while only having net assets to the value of £3 million. A premium of £1 million is paid for the goodwill that exists within the firm.

▓ *TIP* Goodwill can be listed on the balance sheet as an intangible fixed asset. Many companies choose not to do so and will write off any goodwill for which they pay when taking over other businesses.

grapevine: *informal communication* network existing within a business.

▓ This form of communication is often referred to as rumour or gossip and takes place through unofficial channels. The grapevine within a business is likely to develop in the absence of effective methods of *formal communication*.

green audit: see *environmental audit*.

greenfield site: a building site on which construction has not previously taken place.

▓ These are locations, usually outside towns and cities, that are developed for the first time. Such sites are cheap to develop, but firms might experience problems obtaining planning permission to build factories, offices or shops. The UK government encourages businesses to develop 'brownfield sites' — that is, areas in which there has already been construction — in an effort to transform derelict inner-city locations and protect the green belt.

grey market: legal business transactions that take place outside normal business channels.

▓ Grey markets occur when an imbalance exists between supply and demand. If supply exceeds demand, a grey market might develop to offer discounts. Conversely, if demand is greater, goods might be bought in grey markets with purchasers paying a premium for scarce products. Grey markets might also occur when manufacturers charge different prices in different locations for the same product. See also *parallel imports*.

▓ *e.g.* Small UK distributors are purchasing top-brand motorcycles in the Netherlands (where they are much cheaper than the UK) and reselling them in the UK at a substantial profit.

gross national product (GNP): value of all goods and services produced by an economy over a period of time, normally 1 year.

▓ GNP is the value of output produced within the country (gross domestic product, GDP) plus net income earned overseas. GNP can be affected by *inflation*, which exaggerates the value of goods and services produced by an economy. For this reason, real GNP figures are calculated, which remove the effects of inflation. See also *business cycle*.

gross profit: money received from sales less the costs of goods or services sold; other expenses, such as those incurred by administration, are not deducted.

▓ Gross profit is recorded in the trading account within a business's *profit and loss account*. See also *net profit*.

g

■ *TIP* It is important to recognise that several forms of profit exist and to try to use terms such as 'gross profit' precisely, rather than generally referring to 'profits'.

gross profit margin: percentage of a product's selling price that is *gross profit*.

■ It can be measured by the following formula:

$$\text{gross profit margin} = \frac{\text{gross profit}}{\text{sales turnover}} \times 100$$

A higher gross profit margin is preferable to a lower figure, although figures vary considerably between industries. In general, businesses that sell their products quickly have a lower gross profit margin. Thus a jeweller would have a high profit margin, while a supermarket would record a lower figure.

growth: expansion of the production levels of a business or economy over a period of time.

■ For many businesses, growth is an important objective. It offers the possibility of increased profits, perhaps as a result of *economies of scale*, in addition to increased security as survival becomes more assured. Growth in the economy normally results in citizens enjoying a higher standard of living and might lead to increased demand for luxury products.

Handy, Charles: management educator and writer.

■ Handy, born in Dublin in 1932, was a student at Oxford University before becoming a manager with Shell. This was followed by a period as an economist in the City of London. Handy commenced his academic career by joining the London Business School in 1968, becoming Professor of Management Development there in 1972. He is best known for his writing on the structure of organisations and the ways in which they use (or might use) their employees. His books include *Understanding Organizations* (1976), *The Age of Unreason* (1989) and *Inside Organizations* (1990).

Hawthorne effect: the way in which the performance of workers improves when they receive attention from other individuals and groups.

■ This effect was 'discovered' by Elton *Mayo* and other academics from the Harvard Business School during experiments at the Hawthorne plant of Western Electric near Chicago. Testing a group of women, the researchers in turn altered working hours, pay rates, lighting and other conditions. When all the original working conditions were restored, workers' productivity continued to rise. Mayo concluded that the benefits of working in groups and receiving attention from other people were responsible for the improved *motivation* and *productivity*.

■ *TIP* Mayo is an important figure — his theories gave rise to the *human relations* school of management. Many of his ideas lie behind current business practices, such as *teamworking*.

headhunter: someone who recruits employees, normally by persuading them to leave their current employment.

■ Headhunters are usually part of an employment agency hired by businesses to find particular employees for them. This style of *recruitment* is used to appoint executives, senior managers and other employees with highly specialist and rare skills.

headline rate of inflation: see *retail prices index*.

health and safety: aspect of business activity designed to provide all employees with a secure and risk-free working environment.

■ In the UK, legislation exists to ensure that firms conform to rigorous health and safety standards. The central piece of legislation is the Health and Safety Act 1974, which is continuously updated to ensure its relevance to modern working practices. The Health and Safety Executive (HSE) enforces regulations relating to health and safety. Officials from the HSE monitor factories and offices, and investigate serious accidents in the workplace.

Herzberg, Frederick: psychologist and writer on the management of people.

■ Herzberg was born in 1923 in Massachusetts, in the USA. He visited the Dachau concentration camp soon after its liberation and the experiences he had there had a powerful influence on his writings. His central theme is the importance of fulfilling people at work through the process of *job enrichment*. He argues that job enrichment releases the creative energy within people and allows businesses to get the best from their workforces. He taught at Western Reserve University and the University of Utah business school. His books include *The Motivation to Work* (1959) and *Work and the Nature of Man* (1966).

hierarchy of needs: theory that employees have a succession of desires that can be fulfilled through work.

■ Abraham *Maslow* argued that by fulfilling successive levels of an employee's needs, his or her *motivation* can be improved. The lower-level needs are physical and can be met through decent pay and working conditions. Thereafter further improvements in motivation can be achieved by meeting employees' higher needs — those relating to self-esteem, status and the fulfilment of potential.

■ *TIP* Many students are able to describe Maslow's hierarchy of needs and to draw the famous triangle. What relatively few are good at is relating his theory to the circumstances of an examination question. Examiners award most marks for applying the theory, not reproducing it.

hire purchase: means of purchasing goods whereby the buyer pays through a series of instalments over a period of time.

■ In most cases, the goods do not belong to the purchaser until the final payment is made. Because of this, the supplier of the products can reclaim them if the buyer defaults on payments. Purchasing on hire purchase assists a firm's *cash flow* by avoiding the need to raise large sums of capital, but assets purchased this way are likely to be more expensive.

■ *TIP* Do not overestimate the importance of hire purchase. Although mentioned in most textbooks, hire purchase is a much less popular form of credit for consumers nowadays than it used to be. The ready availability and convenience of credit cards has been a major factor in this demise.

historic cost: method of valuing *assets* at their original cost as opposed to the cost of replacing them.

■ An asset might be included on the *balance sheet* at historic cost, but during periods of *inflation* the level of *depreciation* provision made within the accounts might understate the true cost of production and exaggerate the profits made by the company. Managers and shareholders might be misled by inflated profit figures into thinking that the business is performing better than it actually is.

holding company: a company that controls one or more other companies.

■ Under UK law, one company is considered to control another if it holds 50% or more of that company's *shares* or has control of the *board of directors*. Holding companies are common in the UK as a means of growth through acquisition. Companies might purchase other companies to spread their risk through a policy of *diversification*. An intermediate holding company is one that owns a *subsidiary*, but is itself owned by another holding company.

■ *e.g.* General Electric, the giant American corporation, is one of the world's largest holding companies with interests in engineering, construction and life assurance.

horizontal communication (also called 'lateral communication'): exchange of information and ideas between people at similar levels within an organisation.

■ A manager responsible for marketing might need to discuss advertising budgets with the manager of the finance department. Rivalry between individuals and departments at similar levels in organisations means that horizontal communication is not always effective. See also *vertical communication*.

horizontal integration: bringing together two or more businesses in the same industry and at the same stage of production.

■ This type of *integration* offers a number of benefits to businesses, including the elimination of competition and the possibility of achieving significant *economies of scale*. By bringing together organisations with different strengths, the new, larger business can be highly competitive. Horizontal integration might not be in the interests of consumers and may be subject to an investigation by the *Competition Commission*.

■ *e.g.* An example of horizontal integration is the *merger* between the Halifax Building Society and the Leeds Building Society.

horizontal loading: see *job enlargement*.

HRM: see *human resource management*.

human relations: management philosophy that attaches great importance to social interaction and relationships within the workplace.

■ Human relations management seeks to improve employee performance by meeting workers' social needs (and especially the need to belong) and by displaying a concern for the well-being of the individual. It originated from the work of Elton *Mayo* and was popular in the 1950s and 1960s. Human relations management resulted in the development of sports and social facilities within many organisations, the organisation of works outings and other social events, and techniques such as *teamworking*.

human resource management (HRM): making the most efficient use of the organisation's employees.

■ HRM includes the *recruitment, training, motivation* and payment of all staff within a business. It is not simply another term for the activities carried out by the personnel department. *Personnel management* views activities such as recruitment, selection, training and motivation as separate activities. In contrast, human resource management is an integrated approach to managing people that aims to use an organisation's human resources as effectively as possible in pursuit of *corporate objectives*. Human resource management has elevated the management of people within an organisation to a strategic level and one to be controlled by senior managers. This change is in recognition of the importance of people to modern organisations.

hygiene factors (also called 'maintenance factors'): group of influences that might result in employee dissatisfaction at work.

■ Frederick *Herzberg* believed that these factors could not positively motivate employees, but had the potential to demotivate if regarded as inadequate. Thus high levels of pay will not motivate, Herzberg argued, but low rates might damage employee motivation and performance.

■ *e.g.* pay, working conditions and relationships with fellow employees and supervisors.

hypermarket: large supermarket selling a wide range of products and located outside town and city centres.

■ Hypermarkets provide consumers with a huge choice of products, easy access and plenty of parking. Many food retailers (e.g. Sainsbury's and Tesco) sell a large proportion of their products through hypermarkets and have closed many smaller high street supermarkets.

IIP: see *Investors in People.*

import duty: see *tariff.*

imports: purchases of goods and services from suppliers overseas.

◾ Imports are important to the UK, with about one-third of the needs of UK citizens and businesses being met from overseas. To purchase imports, UK inhabitants have to sell pounds sterling and purchase the necessary foreign currency. Buying large volumes of imports results in the sale of considerable quantities of pounds and can result in a decline in the *exchange rate.* The exchange rate might rise if purchases of imports decline.

◾ *e.g.* The UK imports raw materials, *consumer durables* (such as cars) and services (for example, a holiday in Spain) from foreign countries.

impulse purchase: product bought on the spur of the moment without careful planning.

◾ Consumers often purchase relatively inexpensive items (e.g. sweets, magazines and ice creams) on impulse. Firms supplying these products place great emphasis on *point-of-sale* promotion — display stands and packaging might influence consumer purchase decisions. Suppliers of products that are purchased on impulse also seek to distribute their products as widely as possible. If their products are not on display, consumers cannot decide to buy them.

income: money earned from the sale of goods or services.

◾ Income can take a number of forms. Businesses receive income in the form of *sales revenue* from selling their products; they might also earn interest or *dividends* from their investments and rent from the letting of property. For individuals, income is normally the return for selling their labour services. The level of income received by the nation as a whole (*gross national product*) is an important influence for many firms, as sales are likely to be higher during periods of increased incomes. See also *business cycle.*

income elasticity of demand: measures the responsiveness of demand for a product to changes in consumer income.

◾ *e.g.* If demand for foreign holidays increases substantially as a result of a small rise in consumers' incomes, income elasticity of demand for foreign holidays is positive and high. If, at the same time, demand for UK holidays increases marginally, income elasticity of demand for UK holidays is positive but low. Finally, the same small rise in income might result in a fall in demand for public transport (as consumers are more able to afford their own transport), which means that income elasticity of demand for public transport is negative.

The categories of income elasticity

Income elastic	Income inelastic	Negative income elasticity
Percentage rise in demand for a product is **greater** than the percentage increase in income that caused it (e.g. restaurant meals, televisions, computers and CD players).	Percentage rise in demand for a product is **smaller** than the percentage increase in income that caused it (e.g. basic foodstuffs, such as bread and vegetables, washing-up liquid and newspapers).	A rise in income levels leads to a fall in demand for the product in question (e.g. demand for public transport and cheap clothing might decline when incomes increase).

income tax: charge imposed by the government on the earnings of individuals and some small businesses.

▨ The Inland Revenue collects income tax in the UK on behalf of the government. Income tax is charged at variable rates in bands according to the level of income earned. The rates for individual people in 2000/01 were:

Income level (£)	Rate of income tax levied (%)
0–4,385	0
4,385–5,905	10
5,906–34,305	22
34,306 and above	40

The rates of income tax set by the government perform three important functions. First, rates of income tax are an important part of *fiscal policy*. The level of economic activity can be substantially affected by changing the rate of income tax. Second, income tax is an important weapon in redistributing income from richer to less well-off groups in society. Finally, and perhaps most importantly, the government raises money to fund its spending plans through levying income tax.

incorporation: establishing a business that has a separate legal identity from those of its owners.

▨ In the UK, companies are incorporated businesses, having their own legal identity and being able to sign contracts, sue and be sued. The owners of companies (*shareholders*) are separate and not responsible for the debts of the business, benefiting from the privilege of *limited liability*. This privilege means that shareholders can only be held liable for the money they have invested, or have promised to invest, in the business. A business achieves incorporation by completing a *Memorandum of Association* and *Articles of Association* and sending these to the *Registrar of Companies*. In return, it receives a Certificate of Incorporation and can commence trading.

index number: single figure showing the change in a variable such as prices, costs or volumes of output over a period of time.

▓ Index numbers are based on the figure 100, which represents the variable at the start of the period. Thus if wages rise by 7.3% over a 2-year period, 100 would indicate the wage level at the start of the period and 107.3 the wage level after 2 years. Index numbers can represent single items or groups of products known as 'baskets'. See also *weighted index.*

▓ *e.g.* The best-known index number in the UK is the *retail price index* (RPI): by 1998 the RPI stood at 129.8, compared with its base of 100 in 1990.

indirect costs: expenditure not associated with a particular good, service or *cost centre*.

▓ Indirect costs arise as a result of expenditure on buildings, equipment and other items that relate to all aspects of the business's activities. See also *overheads.*

induction: process by which a new employee is integrated into a business.

▓ The major element of induction is normally *training*, which acquaints the employee with the procedures and policies of the firm and provides an introduction to the duties that the individual is expected to carry out.

industrial action: any activity organised by employees or their representatives as part of a protest against an employer during a dispute.

▓ The intention of any form of industrial action is to put pressure on employers to concede to the demands of their employees. In the 1980s, UK governments passed a succession of Acts designed to limited the power of organised labour (*trade unions*). As a result, industrial action has become less common.

▓ *e.g.* strikes, go-slows, work-to-rules and overtime bans.

▓ *TIP* Students tend to think of strikes as the only form of industrial action. However, trade unions tend to use other forms of action first and only call a strike as a last resort.

industrial democracy: participation of employees in the decision-making process of a business.

▓ Industrial democracy can take a number of forms. Workers can be elected to represent their colleagues on the *board of directors*, employees might become *shareholders* and have voting rights at *annual general meetings*, or firms might operate a *works council* — a forum for employees from all levels within the organisation. Some businesses genuinely involve employees in decision making through industrial democracy in the hope of improving employee performance. Others make only a token attempt as a *public relations* exercise.

industrial dispute: disagreement between an employer and employees (or their representatives) over matters such as pay and working conditions.

▓ An industrial dispute might take place over a prolonged period or might be resolved quickly. The *Advisory, Conciliation and Arbitration Service (ACAS)* offers its services to settle disputes and avoid costly *industrial action*.

industrial inertia: when businesses remain in a particular area even though the original reason for their location might have disappeared.

■ *e.g.* The textile industry was first attracted to locate in Lancashire because of its damp climate and its proximity to ports such as Liverpool, through which raw cotton arrived. Today these commercial advantages no longer exist and a textile factory could set up in most regions of the UK.

industrial tribunal: informal court established to hear employees' complaints about their employers.

■ Each tribunal comprises three people: a chair, who has legal training, and two other people, representing employer and employee interests. Tribunals mainly deal with cases where employees claim *unfair dismissal*. Tribunals are located throughout the UK. If a tribunal upholds an employee's case, he or she might receive compensation or be re-engaged by the firm. Recent legislation has substantially increased the levels of compensation to which employees might be entitled.

industrial union: *trade union* that aims to represent all the workers employed in a particular industry.

■ Members of industrial unions normally have the same, or related, skills. The number of industrial unions has declined as a result of a series of mergers between unions.

■ *e.g.* ASLEF (Associated Society of Locomotive Engineers and Firemen) has nearly 15,000 members in the rail industry, working as train drivers, guards and in supervisory roles.

inferior good: product for which demand declines as consumers' incomes rise.

■ Demand for inferior goods falls as incomes rise because consumers alter their spending to purchase products they perceive to be of higher quality. Inferior goods have negative income elasticity. See also *income elasticity of demand*.

■ *e.g.* cheap foodstuffs, public transport and UK-based holidays.

inflation: a sustained rise in the general level of prices and a corresponding fall in the purchasing power of money.

■ Inflation varies in its severity. Creeping inflation describes a situation where prices rise by a few per cent annually, while hyperinflation exists when prices increase at very high rates. Businesses are not averse to low rates of inflation, but higher rates pose considerable difficulties for most firms. Primarily, high rates of inflation in the UK make it difficult for domestic firms to maintain price competitiveness. Inflation is normally measured on an annual basis using the *retail price index*.

■ *TIP* It is important to understand the implications for businesses of periods of inflation and how they might respond. The nature and causes of inflation are of limited relevance and unlikely to attract questions in business studies examinations.

informal communication: exchange of information and ideas using unofficial channels within a business.

- Informal communication can help *formal communication* by facilitating the exchange of information that might not pass through official channels. For instance, a business might learn of a rival's intention to launch a new product.

- *e.g.* Gossip is a prime example of informal communication within a business. However, gossip through the *grapevine* can distort information and might result in misunderstandings.

information technology: use of electronic equipment for storing and exchanging information.

- Businesses have experienced a revolution in information technology over recent years. Increasingly, firms rely upon technology to carry out administrative functions (such as automated switchboards), to construct, store and amend product designs and to control machines completing manufacturing processes.

- *e.g.* One of the most profound developments in information technology has been the development of the *Internet*. See also *computer-aided design* and *computer-aided manufacture*.

- *TIP* There are many positive consequences of developments in information technology. However, it has resulted in many job losses, creates insecurity among employees and requires huge expenditure by businesses on equipment that might be obsolete within a few years.

informative advertising: communicating with potential customers to provide factual information about goods or services.

- Informative advertising is less common than *persuasive advertising* and is likely to be generated by firms producing new, highly technical products.

innovation: introduction by a business of a new product or process.

- Innovation requires the practical application of a new idea into a process or as the basis for a new product. Regular innovation resulting in new products and processes is the cornerstone of a competitive business, but requires heavy expenditure on *research and development* if it is to succeed. Industries such as pharmaceuticals and computer manufacture rely heavily upon innovation.

- *TIP* It is important to use business terms precisely. Invention means the development of a new idea, while innovation is the application of this idea to create a new product or process.

insolvency: when a business is unable to pay its debts as they become due.

- In these circumstances, a business's *liabilities* will exceed its *assets*. It is illegal for an insolvent business to continue trading.

intangible assets: items owned by a business that do not physically exist.

- These are *assets* such as brand names, *goodwill, patents* and *trade marks* that have monetary value. Although this type of asset is not easy to value, it is increasingly common for businesses to include intangible assets on their *balance sheets*. See also *amortisation*.

■ *e.g.* Mobile telephone companies include licences to operate their phone services as intangible assets on their balance sheets and reduce their value over the period of the licence.

integration (also called 'amalgamation'): when two or more businesses join together for their mutual benefit.

■ Integration can take the form of a voluntary *merger* or a *takeover* in which one business gains control of another. A number of different types of integration exist, as shown in the diagram. *Horizontal integration* occurs when two rival companies combine through takeover or merger. *Vertical integration* involves a business joining together with other firms at different stages in the same industry. When two or more firms producing related products, but not in direct competition, join together, this is lateral integration. Finally, conglomerate or diversifying mergers occur when unrelated businesses join together.

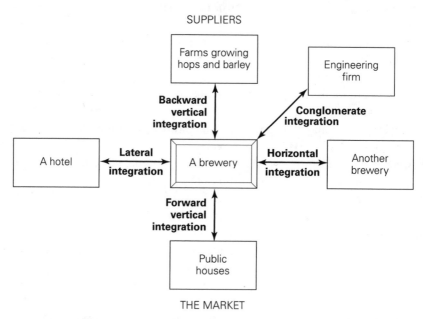

interest cover: compares a company's profits before interest and tax with the interest payments to which it is committed.

■ This is a ratio that calculates the number of times the firm's profits would pay the interest due on its loans.

$$\text{interest cover} = \frac{\text{profit before tax and interest}}{\text{interest paid}}$$

This ratio is of value to a person or business intending to invest in the company concerned, as it provides some indication of the security of their proposed investment. A result of 1 would require a firm to use all its profits to meet its interest charges; a satisfactory interest cover figure would be 4 or 5.

interest rate: the price of borrowed money.

▨ It is common to refer to a single interest rate at any one time, although a variety of rates might be in operation. All interest rates relate to the *base rate* set by the *Bank of England* each month. The precise rates charged in any circumstance depend upon the degree of risk associated with any loan as well as the term or length of the loan. Interest rates are an important weapon used by the authorities to control the economy and to provide a stable economic environment for businesses and consumers.

▨ *TIP* Changes in interest rates do not only affect businesses operating in domestic markets. Variations in interest rates affect a nation's *exchange rate* and hence the prices of exports and imports. This can be a useful line of analysis when answering examination questions.

internal rate of return: that level of return on an *investment* that results in the *net present value* of the investment being equal to zero.

▨ If the internal rate of return is higher than the current rate of interest, the investment should go ahead; if not, it should be abandoned. See also *present value*.

international competitiveness: extent to which a business can match the standards achieved by rival firms from overseas.

▨ Competitiveness has a number of elements. Firms might need to be competitive in terms of price, especially if demand is price elastic. They might also be required at least to equal the standards of foreign producers in terms of quality, design, reliability and delivery dates. Many factors influence a business's ability to compete internationally. Internal factors such as labour productivity are important, but external influences such as changes in the rate of *inflation* and *exchange rates* can have a profound effect upon a firm's ability to compete in international markets.

▨ *TIP* International competitiveness is an important theme in AS and A2 business studies. You should be aware of the factors that contribute to international competitiveness and the implications for firms unable to match their foreign rivals.

International Standards Organisation (ISO): worldwide federation of national standards bodies intended to promote the establishment of common standards in business to assist the international exchange of goods and services.

▨ ISO is a non-governmental organisation established in 1947. The mission of ISO is to promote the development of agreed international standards in relation to product quality, safety and performance. ISO's work results in international agreements published as International Standards.

▨ *e.g.* One of the best-known standards is ISO 9000, which is the worldwide equivalent of BS5750, the UK's major standard for quality assurance.

Internet: worldwide system of linked computer networks which facilitates communication and commercial activities across the globe.

▨ The Internet was originally developed in 1969 for the US army by researchers at the University of California. By 2000, the Internet had linked over 70 million computers throughout the world. The commercial possibilities of the Internet are startling. *E-commerce* (selling products on the Internet) is the most obvious commercial possibility, offering producers the chance to sell their products in international markets — this is sometimes referred to as 'e-tailing'. By July 2000, over 10 million UK citizens had access at home to the Internet.

intervention: the government or another public authority becoming involved in the operation of a market or the activities of a business.

▨ Recent UK governments have reduced the extent of their involvement in the management of the economy, placing greater reliance on *free enterprise* to shape business decisions and actions. In particular, governments have reduced their expenditure on supporting ailing businesses and influencing firms' choices of location.

investment: purchase of *fixed assets* by an organisation.

▨ Investment in fixed assets is essential if a business is to generate profits; without machinery, vehicles and property, a business will not be able to produce goods and services for resale. Businesses plan major investments carefully and undertake substantial forecasting of costs and likely returns before taking a final decision. See also *investment appraisal.*

▨ *TIP* Investment is an important word in business studies. It might refer not only to the purchase of fixed assets, but also to the purchase of *stocks* and *shares*, or even of other businesses. The common theme is that it involves the risk of some resources in pursuit of some gain.

investment appraisal: series of techniques designed to assist businesses in judging the desirability of purchasing particular *fixed assets.*

▨ Investment appraisal can be used to help decide whether to undertake a particular *investment* or to choose between alternative investments. All the major techniques compare the likely costs and returns associated with the investments. More sophisticated techniques, such as *net present value*, also take into account the timing of receipts and payments as well as the rate of interest. See also *average rate of return, internal rate of return* and *payback.*

Investors in People (IIP): national organisation created by the government to assist firms to improve employee performance through more effective use of their employees.

▨ Investors in People (UK) was established in 1993 with the aim of encouraging firms to take a more strategic view of *training* and development. Since then, tens of thousands of UK employers, employing millions of people, have achieved the Investors in People award. Many businesses include the laurel wreath logo on their publicity materials. With the continued growth and take-up of the standard in the UK, international interest has been stimulated and continues to grow.

invisible trade: the purchase and sale of services such as banking on international markets.

- The UK has had a surplus on trade in invisibles (balanced to some extent by a deficit on its *visible trade*) on many occasions in recent years.
- *e.g.* banking, insurance, shipping and tourism.

invoice: document sent from a business to a customer, setting out the details of a purchase and requesting payment.

- Most invoices contain similar information: the name and address of the supplier and customer, the products purchased, the total price plus relevant dates and the date by which payment is due. It is normal for an invoice to be sent once the products have been delivered.

inward investment: flow of capital into one country from individuals or businesses in another country.

- This capital might be invested into fixed assets, as in the case of Honda building a major car factory in Swindon. When making decisions on overseas investment, foreign businesses take into account factors such as labour and other costs, the skills existing in the workforce, proximity to markets and the extent of government support. The UK is the most successful country in Europe in attracting investment from foreign-owned companies. Foreign-owned firms employ nearly one-fifth of the labour force in UK manufacturing industry, produce nearly one-quarter of UK output and were responsible for almost one-third of all UK capital investment.
- *e.g.* Inward investment led to the creation of Nissan's car manufacturing plant at Sunderland.

ISO: see *International Standards Organisation*.

issued share capital: the amount of its *authorised share capital* that a company has actually sold to its *shareholders*.

- *e.g.* A company might be entitled to raise £100 million through the sale of shares, but if it has only sold shares to the value of £60 million, this latter figure is its issued capital. At an *annual general meeting*, shareholders can decide to increase a company's issued share capital, but not its authorised share capital.
- *TIP* The issue of extra shares (increasing the company's issued share capital) might raise more money than the face value of the shares indicates. Thus if a company sells an extra 10 million shares with a face (or nominal) value of £1 each, the sum raised might exceed £10 million if the market price of the company's shares is greater than £1 each.

Japanisation: steady adoption of Japanese management techniques by businesses in the UK and other western countries.

- Japanisation encompasses a number of management techniques, including those relating to the workforce (e.g. *kaizen*) as well as *lean production* techniques designed to use resources more efficiently (e.g. *just-in-time* production). The adoption of these methods of management has been accelerated by the success of Japanese companies such as Sony and Nissan and their decisions to locate manufacturing plants in the UK.

- *TIP* It is important to appreciate that UK companies have only adopted selective management techniques employed in Japanese firms. Many Japanese firms offer secure lifetime employment and pay wages according to length of service; UK firms have not chosen to implement these approaches.

JIT: see *just-in-time*.

job description: document setting out the duties and tasks associated with a particular post.

- Job descriptions are normally sent to candidates prior to interview and are often incorporated into a contract of employment. See also *job specification*.

job design: amalgamating tasks and duties to form a complete job.

- Non-monetary methods of motivation tend to focus on the design of employees' jobs. Several writers on *motivation*, notably *Herzberg*, argue that employee performance can be improved through the design (or redesign) of jobs to offer employees more challenging and complex duties. A good job should allow employees to carry out duties that have a definite end product, provide employees with clear and challenging goals, and offer them some degree of control over their working lives. See also *job enlargement* and *job enrichment*.

job enlargement (also called 'horizontal loading'): redesigning a job to include additional tasks of a similar level of complexity.

- This approach to *job design* might offer limited *motivation* to employees, but it is unlikely to make the job more challenging — just busier!

- *e.g.* A receptionist might be required to undertake some book-keeping tasks as well as dealing with telephone and personal enquiries from customers.

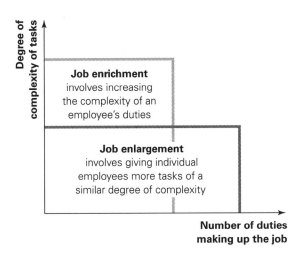

job enrichment: redesigning a job to include more challenging and complex duties.

▨ The intention of job enrichment is to offer employees greater authority in the workplace and to make their working lives more rewarding. As a consequence, businesses hope for improved employee performance. *Herzberg* is a strong advocate of job enrichment, believing that redesigning a job to provide employees with motivators is a key element in successful management of the workforce. Job enrichment is likely to require firms to implement a major policy of *training* to provide employees with the necessary skills to carry out their new jobs effectively.

▨ *TIP* Job enrichment is an important topic in business studies and is the principle underpinning techniques of management such as *empowerment* and *teamworking*.

job evaluation: systematic rating of all jobs within an organisation, taking into account the skills and experience needed and the degree of responsibility involved.

▨ Job evaluation, although an expensive process to complete, provides a logical basis for determining the pay structure (but not the pay rates) of the organisation by assessing the value of particular posts to the business. It attempts to ensure that the relationship between rates of pay for different jobs is seen to be fair. Jobs requiring greater amounts of skill, experience and responsibility will receive higher rates of pay. The results of job evaluation can be particularly useful when resolving disputes over pay, especially equal pay claims.

job production: method of production in which a product is supplied in response to a specific order from a customer.

▨ Job production can increase consumers' satisfaction as products meet their requirements precisely. However, using job production with highly technical products can result in consumers facing high prices, as *economies of scale* cannot be gained. See also *batch production* and *mass production*.

■ *e.g.* In the catering industry, food and drinks are supplied to meet individual customer requirements. The construction industry engages in job production, from building an extension to a house, to the design and assembly of the Millennium Bridge across the River Thames in London.

job rotation: regular switching of employees between tasks of a similar degree of complexity.

■ Job rotation is a particular form of *job enlargement*. It is commonly used on *production lines* to alleviate the monotony associated with repeating relatively simple tasks. In this respect, job rotation has had limited success because employees regard it as 'more of the same'. Some firms use job rotation with trainee managers, switching them between departments to give them an appreciation of the whole organisation, and to prepare them for more senior roles.

job specification (also called 'person specification'): document listing the qualities and qualifications sought in applications for a particular job.

■ A job specification might list the relevant experience required and the personal qualities wanted (e.g. an ability to work as part of a team, good communication skills) as well as educational and vocational qualifications sought. It might list some qualities and qualifications as essential and others as desirable. The job specification forms an important part of the selection process, as the candidates for a position can be judged against the specification in order to select the best applicant. See also *job description*.

just-in-case: production system in which a firm holds some quantities of raw materials and finished goods to meet demand as it arises.

■ This method of *stock control* used to be common in most industries, ensuring that firms were always able to meet customers' demands. Under this system, stock levels are based on historical production and demand patterns. The influence of Japanese firms on UK manufacturing has now led to the widespread adoption of *just-in-time* production methods.

just-in-time (JIT): production system under which raw materials, partly manufactured goods and finished products are delivered at the precise time they are required.

■ JIT entails coordinating the supply of materials and components with production to eliminate the need to hold *buffer stocks*. The principal aim of JIT methods is to reduce waste by using minimal amounts of materials, parts, factory or office space and workers' time. JIT is a 'pull' production system, under which demand instigates production. Finished goods are produced just in time to be supplied to the consumer, and components and materials arrive just in time to be used in the production process. In this way, production takes place without the need to hold stocks. This can be highly cost efficient, but it requires reliable suppliers who will deliver materials and components on time. See also *kanban*.

■ *TIP* JIT is not simply a *stock control* system; it is a complete production system that aims to achieve continuous improvement within the firm rather than merely minimising stock-holding costs.

kaizen: management philosophy that aims at continuous improvement in all aspects of the operation of a business.

■ Kaizen entails small but continual advances in methods of working, each one improving *productivity* in some way. It is an important part of the Japanese approach to management and is at the heart of *lean production*. Kaizen encourages workers to suggest ideas to improve the way a business operates, leading to a series of small improvements in the way production takes place. Kaizen groups might be formed to encourage suggestions and ideas from all workers. The small continuous changes that lie at the heart of the kaizen approach are unlikely to require major capital expenditure by businesses, but help maintain competitiveness.

■ *TIP* Kaizen relates to an enormous range of business activities, not just production. For example, improvements can be achieved through kaizen in customer service, training methods and internal communication.

kanban: system used within *just-in-time* production to ensure that materials are ordered promptly.

■ Under this system, materials and components are pulled through the production process by cards, known as kanban. Kanban are attached to containers designed to hold materials and components. It is the kanban themselves that stimulate production — without them no production will occur. Kanban thereby control and limit the amount of production in the system.

Keynes, John Maynard: English economist who founded a school of thought (called Keynesian economics) that advocated government intervention in the economy to manage the level of activity.

■ Keynes believed that the government should control the level of spending in the economy by firms, individuals and, importantly, the government itself. He argued that such management could control the worst excesses of the *business cycle* and thus *unemployment* and *inflation*. Keynes was born in 1883 and spent considerable periods of time as an economic adviser to the government as well as holding an academic position at King's College, Cambridge. Keynes was involved in establishing the International Monetary Fund in 1944.

knowledge management: the requirement on firms to ensure that their employees have sufficient skills, experience and knowledge to allow the organisation to perform effectively.

■ This is an important part of *human resource management* with significant implications for *recruitment* and *training*. Knowledge management has become a key issue for businesses as a result of techniques such as *delayering* and *rationalisation*, which have led to many experienced employees being made redundant. In some cases, firms have been unable to function effectively following drastic shakeouts of labour.

labour: the human element within production.

▨ Labour includes all forms of human activity within a business, whether mental or physical. For economists, labour is one of the *factors of production* (along with land, capital and enterprise).

labour intensive: method of production that relies heavily upon human resources.

▨ A firm that is labour intensive will have wages and salaries as a high proportion of its costs and use relatively little capital and land in production. Many businesses providing services (e.g. education, health, and painting and decorating) rely heavily upon labour and use relatively little capital equipment in the production process. Businesses might choose to be labour intensive because labour is relatively cheap compared to other factors of production such as capital. See also *capital intensive*.

▨ *e.g.* education and the National Health Service.

labour market: market in which individuals seek employment and organisations recruit workers.

▨ This market operates throughout the UK and to an increasing extent is influenced by events in Europe and the rest of the world. For example, the UK market for professional footballers attracts individuals from most countries in the world. If individuals are unable to find work then *unemployment* is the result; if firms are unable to recruit then *vacancies* are said to exist. The government, through its network of job centres, attempts to bring together those seeking work and potential employers. Various private firms (recruitment agencies) carry out similar functions.

▨ *TIP* Many textbooks refer to the labour market as if only one existed. In reality there are many. Labour markets can be local, relating to a particular geographical area; they can also be occupational, such as the labour market for engineers.

labour mobility: measures the freedom with which employees can move between businesses, occupations and geographical areas.

▨ It is normal for employees to seek to move in pursuit of higher wages. The movement of labour between different firms in the same industry or between occupations might be the result of differences in pay, conditions, training or long-term prospects. Geographical mobility of labour occurs as people seek to further their careers or as a consequence of firms relocating. Labour mobility tends to be higher if information about other jobs and careers is freely available and if people are able to move home without hindrance.

labour turnover: proportion of firm's staff leaving their employment over a period of time, normally a year.

▨ Labour turnover is measured by the following formula:

$$\text{labour turnover} = \frac{\text{number of staff leaving during a year}}{\text{average number of staff employed}} \times 100\%$$

Poor *working conditions*, low *wages* and inadequate *training*, leading to demotivated staff, might cause high levels of labour turnover. Alternatively, high rates of turnover might be a consequence of poor *recruitment* procedures, leading to the appointment of unsuitable staff. Firms require a certain level of labour turnover to bring in new ideas. However, high rates of labour turnover can be harmful, as high expenditure on training and recruitment might be required and the workforce might lack experience.

laissez-faire: philosophy supporting minimal government *intervention* in the economy.

▨ The term 'laissez-faire' means 'leave alone' and is based on the idea that businesses should be able to trade without interference from the government or other authorities. Supporters of laissez-faire believe that businesses are most likely to prosper in an environment in which markets can work as freely as possible.

▨ *TIP* 'Laissez-faire' is also used in connection with *leadership* styles. A laissez-faire leader has a minimal involvement with his or her subordinates, allowing them considerable independence.

last in, first out (LIFO): system of valuing stocks of raw materials and finished goods in which items that are bought earliest are judged to be used last during an *accounting period*.

▨ Any remaining stock is valued at the cost incurred at the start of the accounting period. The use of LIFO for *stock valuation* gives a high cost of production as the costs are based on the latest figure paid for stocks of raw materials and components. As a result, the firm's profits are reduced (on paper at least) and so is its liability to pay income tax or corporation tax. LIFO also tends to undervalue holdings of stocks.

▨ *TIP* The Inland Revenue only accepts certain methods of stock valuation: it approves *first in, first out*, but not the LIFO method of stock valuation, in spite of its benefits to businesses in periods of inflation.

lateral communication: see *horizontal communication*.

latest finish time (LFT): measurement used in *critical path analysis* to indicate the time by which an activity must be completed if the entire project is not to be delayed.

Latest finish times are normally calculated by working backwards through a network and are recorded in the bottom right-hand quadrant of nodes. Calculating latest finish times is useful because it shows the activities in the project in which there is some spare time or float. See also *earliest start time*.

leadership: functions of ruling, guiding and inspiring other people within an organisation in pursuit of agreed objectives.

Leadership is an important element in a successful organisation, but disagreement exists concerning what makes a good leader. Some writers on business studies believe that good leaders are born, while others argue that suitable training can create effective leaders. See also *authoritarian leadership, democratic leadership* and *paternalistic leadership*.

TIP A manager differs from a leader: a manager sets *objectives* and uses resources as efficiently as possible, while a leader motivates people and brings out the best in them to attain *corporate objectives*.

lead time: interval between the placing of an order and the arrival of the goods.

Lead times influence the amount of *buffer stock* held by a business and the timing of the orders. Short lead times allow businesses to hold low levels of stocks and to delay orders until the last minute. They can reduce the costs of holding stocks. See also *stock control*.

lean production: series of management techniques intended to make efficient use of resources in an organisation, thereby minimising waste.

Lean production might entail the use of *kaizen, just-in-time* production techniques and *benchmarking*. Businesses using lean production techniques require multi-skilled workers who are able to carry out a variety of activities. They should be committed to producing goods of high quality continuously and be highly responsive to consumers' needs. Lean production produces what the consumer wants, when it is wanted, using as few resources as possible. This contrasts with the approach of *mass production*.

leasing: hiring of items such as machinery and vehicles for a specified period of time, usually for 2 years or more.

By using leasing, firms can employ *assets* without investing large amounts of capital. Leasing is of particular value when acquiring assets that might rapidly become obsolete, such as computer-based technology. Many firms also lease vehicles and photocopiers because they can get maintenance contracts as part of the deal. One drawback of leasing is that items used in this way do not belong to the business and so do not appear on its *balance sheet*.

levels of hierarchy: number of layers of authority in an organisation.

The trend in modern businesses is to reduce the number of levels of hierarchy through *delayering* to improve communication and offer shop-floor employees more control over their working lives. See also *span of control*.

e.g. In the 1970s, before any delayering, the American motor manufacturer General Motors had an *organisational structure* containing 29 levels of hierarchy!

LFT: see *latest finish time*.

liabilities: money owed by a business to individuals, suppliers, financial institutions and shareholders.

■ All businesses incur liabilities to raise capital to finance their establishment and ongoing operation. Liabilities are recorded on a business's *balance sheet*. They can fall into two categories: amounts owed to external parties such as suppliers and banks (*current liabilities* and *long-term liabilities*); and the amount remaining to owners once external debts have been paid (owners' funds).

■ *TIP* Businesses should not incur liabilities without careful thought and planning. It is not uncommon for businesses to expand rapidly without arranging how they might pay the short-term debts that they will incur as a result of purchasing additional material and labour services. See *overtrading*.

LIFO: see *last in, first out.*

limited liability: restricts the financial responsibility of *shareholders* for a company's debts to the amount they have individually invested.

■ Limited liability makes companies separate, in a legal sense, from their owners and means that companies are responsible for their own debts. In the event of the failure of a company, its shareholders' loss will not exceed the sum they have invested. Some organisations (e.g. cooperatives) limit the liability of their members by guarantee. In these circumstances, the members' liability is restricted to the amount they have guaranteed to contribute in the event of the business being wound up. See also *unlimited liability*.

line manager: employee responsible for a number of subordinates in an organisation.

■ A line manager is normally part of the chain of command extending from the chief executive of the business to the most junior employees. The term is also used to refer to managers who have responsibility for employees carrying out the primary function of the business (e.g. production in a manufacturing business). Line managers are distinct from staff managers, who have authority over people carrying out supporting functions (e.g. the manager of the finance department).

liquid assets: items owned by a business that can easily and quickly be converted into *cash*.

■ It is important for a business to hold a sufficient proportion of its assets in a liquid form, to ensure that it can pay bills as they fall due. However, a firm should not have too many liquid assets because, unlike *fixed assets*, they do not generate profits. See also *current assets* and *liquidity*.

■ *e.g.* *debtors* and money held in bank accounts.

liquidation (also called 'winding up'): dissolution of a company through the sale of its *assets* and the settling of its *liabilities*.

■ Liquidation can be voluntary or compulsory depending upon circumstances. The process is overseen by a liquidator, who arranges for the assets to be sold and for the money realised to be shared among the company's *creditors*. If there are insufficient funds to pay everyone their full amount, creditors receive a set proportion of what they are owed, although certain creditors, such as the Inland Revenue, are given preference.

■ *TIP* Liquidation can follow a company being declared *insolvent*. If an individual or an unincorporated business becomes insolvent, the next stage is *bankruptcy*.

liquidity: percentage of a business's *assets* that are held in a form easily convertible into *cash*.

■ Liquidity measures a business's ability to pay its debts on time. Suppliers and creditors (e.g. banks) will scrutinise a firm's liquidity to determine whether they will be paid promptly. A firm is liquid if it holds a sufficient proportion of *liquid assets*. Businesses should avoid being too liquid as this might damage their profitability by limiting investment in *fixed assets*, which are essential to generate profits. See also *liquidity ratio*.

liquidity ratio (also called 'current ratio')**:** measure of a business's ability to meet its short-term debts.

■ It is calculated by use of the following formula:

$$\text{liquidity ratio} = \frac{\text{current assets}}{\text{current liabilities}}$$

A healthy business would expect a liquidity ratio of approximately 2. This means that for every £1 of short-term debt, the business has £2 available in a relatively liquid form. The reason for holding £2 of *current assets* for each £1 of *current liabilities* is that some current assets (notably *stock*) can be difficult to convert into cash, and so companies need a margin of safety.

■ *TIP* Some businesses operate with a much lower liquidity ratio than 2. For example, supermarkets are normally paid promptly by customers and are therefore confident that they will have cash available to settle their debts.

loan capital: funds used in a business that have been borrowed from external sources such as banks.

■ Individuals and organisations providing loan capital normally expect a fixed interest payment in return for their investment, but they do not receive a share of the firm's profits. Raising capital through loans can be relatively cheap because interest on loans is not subject to tax. However, firms raising large proportions of their capital through loans might become vulnerable to increases in *interest rates*, especially at times when their profits are low. See also *gearing* and *share capital*.

■ *e.g.* debentures and mortgages.

location: site or sites on which a business is based.

■ Major influences on firms' location decisions are proximity to the *market*, to suppliers and to suitably skilled labour. Most firms seek a location or locations in which they can produce at the lowest possible cost.

■ *e.g.* Some businesses operate from a single location, such as the Royal Mint and the Natural History Museum, while others have many locations, such as Woolworth's and Barclays Bank.

■ *TIP* Many businesses sell in global markets and are not, therefore, necessarily restricted to the UK when deciding upon a location. You should consider an international dimension in questions about location.

logistics: science of getting materials, components and finished goods to the right place at the right time.

■ This is an important part of *production* and *distribution*. Some businesses specialise in providing logistics solutions for other firms.

long-term liabilities: debts that a business does not expect to repay within 1 year.

■ Businesses avoid raising too high a proportion of their assets in the form of long-term liabilities, as the interest payments can become burdensome in periods of low profits. See also *gearing* and *liquidity*.

■ *e.g.* debentures and *mortgages*.

loss: amount by which a business's expenditure exceeds its earnings over some period of time.

■ A business might survive a short-term loss (e.g. during the first year or two of its existence). However, in the long term it is unlikely that a loss-making business will survive. Such businesses might be subject to a *takeover* or forced to close down. See also *profit* and *break even*.

■ *e.g.* Many of the Internet-based businesses, such as Amazon.com, recorded losses during their early years of trading.

loss leader: product sold at a price below its cost of production in the hope of attracting consumers to purchase other, standard-price products.

■ *e.g.* Nightclubs and public houses offer cheap drinks (on which they make a loss) early in the evening, hoping that customers will stay for the entire evening and buy a number of full-price drinks. Supermarkets often locate loss leaders at the back of the store, offering customers the fullest opportunity to buy profitable items.

Ltd: see *private limited company*.

McGregor, Douglas: lecturer and management theorist.

■ McGregor changed management practices as a result of his theories on how leaders view their workforces. He was born in Detroit in the USA and taught psychology and industrial management at the Massachusetts Institute of Technology. His *Human Side of Enterprise* (1960) changed American management practices by developing *Theory Y*, a very human view of behaviour and motivation, in contrast to the traditional *Theory X* view of workers as lazy, unmotivated and needing strict control.

■ *e.g.* McGregor's views on leadership were put into practice with notable success at Procter & Gamble's factory in Georgia.

■ *TIP* It is important to recognise that McGregor's ideas are not theories of motivation, but consider two ways in which leaders view their workforce. He argued that the way in which leaders view their employees (whether Theory X or Theory Y) will affect how they treat their workers and the likely performance of their labour force.

macroeconomics: study of the economy as a whole.

■ Macroeconomics covers issues such as *unemployment, inflation* and the rate of *economic growth*. It considers how these variables are determined and how the government might control them. A major aspect of macroeconomics is the government's management of the economy using weapons such as *monetary policy* and *fiscal policy*. See also *Keynes* and *microeconomics*.

maintenance factors: see *hygiene factors*.

management: planning, organising and controlling a business enterprise.

■ Management encompasses a large number of activities, including setting *corporate objectives*, directing employees, co-ordinating the production and selling of goods and services, and monitoring organisational performance in achieving agreed objectives. Management requires the efficient use of resources, in contrast to *leadership*, which focuses on getting the best out of a workforce.

management buy-in: when a management team unconnected with a business purchases sufficient shares to control the enterprise.

■ Management buy-ins can bring much needed entrepreneurial skills to a business as well as access to further capital. However, they are relatively unusual.

■ *e.g.* A management team purchased control of United Biscuits in spring 2000 for over £1.3 billion.

management buy-out: when a company's senior managers purchase sufficient shares to control the business for which they work.

■ Management buy-outs occur when a large firm decides to sell off one part of its organisation or when a business is in financial trouble, but the managers consider it to have potential. It is common for managers to seek financial support from venture capitalists to raise sufficient capital to carry through their plans. A critical element determining the success of a management buy-out is the price paid for the business. If it is too high, interest payments can cripple the fledgling business.

■ *e.g.* An example of a successful management buy-out is the purchase of Electra Investment Trust by its management team. EIT invests pension funds for major companies, including General Electric.

management by objectives (MBO): style of management popularised by Peter Drucker, which emphasises the central role of *objectives* for all managers in an organisation.

■ Drucker argued that senior managers should have a clear understanding of the organisation's overall objectives. From this, a hierarchy of objectives can be developed so that managers at all levels in the organisation have clear aims and contribute to the common goal. For MBO to succeed, managers must contribute to the setting of the objectives that they are to pursue.

management consultant: person or organisation that advises businesses on a range of strategic issues.

■ Management consultants investigate current business practices and offer recommendations. They might also offer professional support in the form of training. Management consultants investigate issues such as *restructuring* the organisation, developing its product range and *rationalisation*. All such investigations are likely to have the objective of increasing profits. Management consultants are employed for their expertise and because they can be objective in their recommendations, having no direct connection with the business.

manpower planning: forecasting a business's likely future labour requirements and comparing these with the employees currently available to the business.

■ Manpower planning specifies the quantity of workers needed as well as the skills they will require. This is then compared with the human resources currently available to the firm. Any mismatch between the firm's future demand for labour and the supply of employees available to it will be rectified by *recruitment, redundancy, redeployment* and retraining as necessary. An important element of manpower planning is the use of a skills audit of the labour force to identify any unknown skills or talents within the workforce.

■ *TIP* Manpower planning integrates the various aspects of managing the labour force and therefore fits in with the philosophy of *human resource management* (as opposed to *personnel management*).

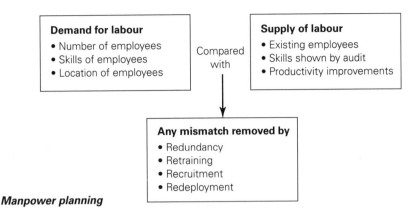

<table>
<tr>
<td>

Demand for labour
- Number of employees
- Skills of employees
- Location of employees

</td>
<td>Compared with</td>
<td>

Supply of labour
- Existing employees
- Skills shown by audit
- Productivity improvements

</td>
</tr>
</table>

Any mismatch removed by
- Redundancy
- Retraining
- Recruitment
- Redeployment

Manpower planning

manufacturing resource planning: information system designed to integrate the planning, scheduling and control of all resources used in production.

■ Manufacturing resource planning uses *information technology* to model the entire *production* process. This model forms the basis on which managers forecast the firm's use of materials, components, machinery and labour, ensuring they are available when required and in the right quantities. The technique can also be used to advise customers of likely delivery dates, given the resources available to the business. There are a number of approaches to manufacturing resource planning, all operating under the same general principles. The best known is MRPII, or manufacturing resource planning, mark two.

margin of safety: amount by which a business's current level of production exceeds the level required to break even.

■ This allows firms to judge by how much their production and sales can decline before they begin to incur a *loss*. See also *break even*.

market: where buyers and sellers come together to trade information and products.

■ Markets take a number of forms. They exist in a geographical form where buyers and sellers meet physically. Other markets, both national and international, exist without a designated physical location.

■ *e.g.* Geographical markets include those held in many towns and cities as well as famous markets such as Smithfield (livestock) and Hatton Garden (jewellery). An example of a product traded in a market without a specified location is oil. This product is bought and sold across the globe with the majority of major transactions taking place by telephone, fax or electronically. Even when consumers purchase oil for personal consumption, they do so in millions of locations worldwide.

market-based pricing: method of pricing dependent upon factors such as consumer demand and competitors' reactions.

■ Market-based pricing suggests that firms will charge higher prices when demand is strong, as happens when travel companies increase prices during school holidays. Equally, this approach to pricing takes into account the likely responses of competitors. Firms might go along with the current market price, not wishing to start a *price war* by selling products at a lower price.

market economy: economy in which businesses are subject to minimal government interference.

In market economies, businesses decide what they are to produce and the price at which they will sell their products. They are motivated in such decisions by self-interest: the desire to make the highest possible profit. In reality, most economies in the world are *mixed economies*, meaning that businesses within them are subject to some intervention by governments (e.g. consumer and employment protection legislation). Over the last 20 years or so, the number of businesses directly owned and managed by governments has declined, partly due to the worldwide implementation of *privatisation*.

market failure: when a market does not work effectively and resources are not allocated properly.

Markets can fail to work properly for a number of reasons. First, the existence of *monopolies* and *cartels* might mean that producers have too much power, resulting in insufficient output and high prices. Second, producers do not bear the full costs of production, so society bears some costs (e.g. pollution and noise). Third, consumers and producers possess insufficient information about products. Consumers might underestimate their need for certain goods (e.g. health and education), resulting in inadequate supply without government intervention in such markets.

TIP Market failure is a strong argument for government *intervention* in the economy and can provide a powerful line of analysis when responding to questions on the merits (or otherwise) of state involvement in the business environment.

marketing: 'the management process that identifies, anticipates and supplies customer requirements efficiently and profitably' (Chartered Institute of Marketing).

Marketing encompasses a number of business activities, including *market research, product design*, pricing, *advertising* and *promotion, customer service, distribution, packaging* and after-sales service. Most employees are involved with marketing in some way. Some Japanese firms do not operate separate marketing departments, emphasising through the structure of the organisation that marketing is the responsibility of all employees.

TIP Marketing is often defined too narrowly. Some students think it is really only advertising and perhaps promotion, whereas its scope is much wider.

marketing mix: combination of four major tools of *marketing* (price, product, *promotion* and *place*) used by a business to influence the behaviour of consumers.

The marketing mix is commonly referred to as the 4Ps. It is important for firms to select the correct mix for their product and the market in which they trade. Thus a firm might emphasise the exclusivity and quality of its products by setting high prices and restricting the number of outlets in which they are available — luxury cars might use this type of mix. Conversely, a firm selling in a highly competitive market might rely upon low prices and heavy advertising — basic groceries are often sold in this way. Some textbooks refer to the 5Ps, or even 6Ps, including *packaging* and people.

■ *TIP* Many examination candidates hope for questions on the marketing mix but do not make the best of the opportunity when it arises. It is tempting to write descriptively about the elements that make up the mix rather than applying the theory to the question. Examiners are unlikely to ask for a description of the marketing mix.

marketing model: structure outlining the process by which marketing decisions can be taken on a scientific basis.

■ This model developed from Frederick *Taylor*'s scientific approach to decision making. The process outlined in the diagram is continuous.

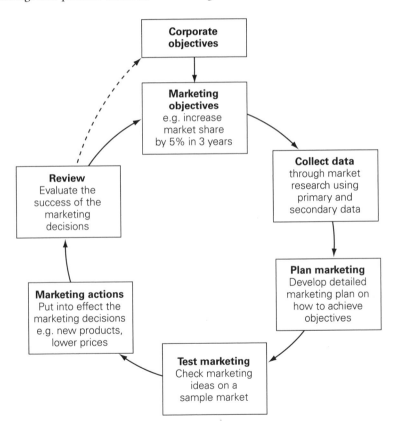

marketing objectives: aims that a business hopes to achieve through its marketing actions.

■ Marketing objectives are usually quantified and given a timescale to provide a more explicit target for businesses (e.g. a 10% increase in market share over

2 years). Marketing objectives should assist an organisation in achieving its *corporate objectives* and are attained through the implementation of a *marketing strategy*.

■ *e.g.* a figure for growth in market share; a target level of profitability from a product line or lines; a forecast cash flow (this might be particularly important for new products).

marketing plan: document setting out the strategies by which a business will achieve its *marketing objectives*.

■ The plan will include details of target markets, tactics such as advertising and promotions to be used, timescales and resources available to those responsible for marketing. A marketing plan for a large organisation might bring together a number of separate marketing plans for individual goods and services.

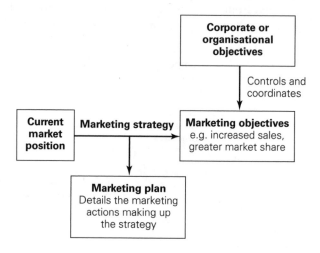

marketing strategy: means by which an organisation intends to attain its *marketing objectives*.

■ Important elements in most marketing strategies are the *marketing mix* to be employed and the *market segment* that the firm is targeting. Large businesses might use different marketing strategies for each of their products. Factors such as the actions of competitors and the type of consumer at which the firm is aiming will be major influences on a business's marketing strategy. See also *market penetration*.

■ *TIP* It is important to understand not only the terms 'marketing plan', 'marketing objectives' and 'marketing strategy', but also the way in which they interrelate.

market orientation: where a business considers the needs of consumers when planning and implementing its marketing activities.

■ Market-orientated businesses exist to discover and meet consumers' needs. Market orientation requires that considerable emphasis be placed on *market research* to identify consumers' desires. However, market-orientated firms must place the interests of consumers at the heart of everything they do. Their employees should acknowledge the importance of meeting consumers' needs and contribute to this by, for example, providing consistently excellent *customer service*.

market penetration: policy designed to increase *sales volume* in the business's existing markets.

■ Market penetration normally involves taking customers from competitors by using aggressive marketing tactics (e.g. reducing prices and/or increasing advertising). Market penetration is one of the opportunities available to a business with *Ansoff's matrix*. See also *penetration pricing*.

market positioning: placing of one business's brand in the market relative to brands of other businesses.

■ Positioning is created in the minds of the target group of consumers by using advertising and promotion to give the product a distinct image. The factors by which a product is positioned depend upon the nature of the product and its market. *Product differentiation* is very important in the process of positioning to ensure that its image differs from that of competitors' products.

■ *e.g.* The motor car manufacturer Skoda is using advertising and PR (participating in rally races) to reposition its products in the minds of consumers who might be sceptical about its quality.

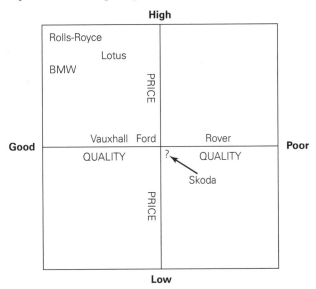

A hypothetical map of the motor car market

market price: price charged for a good or service as a result of the free operation of the forces of demand and supply.

■ Market prices are determined without government intervention. In general, if demand for a product exceeds the supply, the product's market price will rise to restrict demand to supplies available. Conversely, if supply exceeds demand, the price will fall sufficiently to ensure that all supplies of the product find a purchaser. However, sometimes markets do not work effectively and market prices do not send out the right signals. See *market failure*.

market research: systematic collection and analysis of data which enables a business to improve the quality of its marketing decisions.

■ Market research collects information about the needs, preferences, opinions and lifestyles of its potential consumers. As a consequence, firms are better able to design products to meet consumers' actual (as opposed to their anticipated) needs, charge the 'right' price, distribute the product to the correct places and promote the product in an effective manner.

■ *e.g.* Firms undertake two major types of market research: *field research* using questionnaires and interviews; and *desk research* using existing information such as company reports.

market segmentation: division of potential consumers into groups with similar characteristics.

■ Markets might be segmented according to similarities in demographic features (age, sex and social class), psychographics (attitudes and lifestyles) and geography (e.g. which region of the UK consumers inhabit). Segmentation of markets can increase a business's profitability by allowing goods and services to be designed to meet the needs of consumers precisely, by assisting firms in using the optimal marketing techniques and by helping them to identify new market segments.

■ *e.g.* Manufacturers of breakfast cereals, such as Kellogg's, sell their products in several pack sizes to meet the requirements of different market segments, ranging from those living alone to large families.

market share: percentage of the total volume of sales achieved by a firm in a particular market.

■ The market could be local, national or international. Market share is an important indicator of the success of a brand or range of products, and the trends in market share are closely analysed by marketing departments. Increases in market share allow a firm to benefit from *economies of scale*. The firm holding the largest share of a particular market is termed the market leader.

■ *e.g.* Microsoft has over 90% of worldwide sales of software for personal computers.

market structure: how a particular market is organised in terms of the number of suppliers and the degree of competition within it.

■ Some market structures (e.g. *monopolies*) can be relatively uncompetitive, whereas perfectly competitive markets are characterised by intense competition. Competition between firms in a market can be in the form of price, product differentiation and promotional activities. See also *oligopoly*.

■ *TIP* The structure of a market in which the firm is selling is an important influence on its marketing activities. For example, many firms trading in an oligopolistic market avoid price competition for fear of instigating a price war.

mark-up: amount of profit earned from the sale of a good or service as a percentage of the cost of that product.

■ A mark-up is normally expressed as a percentage of the cost of production, but it can also relate to a percentage of the selling price.

■ *e.g.* A furniture retailer purchases a chair for £200 and adds a mark-up of £150 to give a selling price of £350.

$$\text{mark-up as a \% of cost} = \frac{\text{mark-up}}{\text{cost price}} \times 100 = \frac{150}{200} \times 100 = 75\%$$

$$\text{mark-up as a \% of selling price} = \frac{\text{mark-up}}{\text{selling price}} \times 100 = \frac{150}{350} \times 100 = 42.86\%$$

■ *TIP* If you are asked to calculate mark-up as part of a question, it is important to be clear which type of mark-up you are required to provide.

Maslow, Abraham: psychologist born in New York City.

■ Maslow was a professor at Brooklyn College and Brandeis University. He is best known for his *hierarchy of needs*, a theory explaining the successive factors required to motivate people in the workplace. Maslow wrote two major books outlining his theories, *Motivation and Personality* (1954) and *Toward a Psychology of Being* (1962). His papers, published posthumously, were issued in 1971 as *The Farther Reaches of Human Nature*.

mass market: a market containing large numbers of consumers, often purchasing similar products.

■ Competition within mass markets can be fierce (and is often based on price), with businesses aiming to increase market share to generate higher sales and greater profits. Mass markets offer firms the potential to benefit from *economies of scale*, allowing for greater price competitiveness. See also *niche market*.

■ *e.g.* Cars, groceries and *consumer durables* (such as televisions and washing machines) are all sold in mass markets. Some products (such as mobile telephones) were originally sold in niche markets, but are now part of a mass market.

■ *TIP* Firms selling in mass markets are likely to use substantially different approaches to production and marketing. Questions asking how firms might adapt when moving from niche to mass markets are common.

mass production: manufacture of large quantities of uniform products, normally through the use of a *production line*.

■ Mass production originated in the USA in the nineteenth century. It offers low costs for producing a single unit of production and allows firms to set competitive prices. The drawbacks of the system include little variation in products and monotonous roles for employees. These drawbacks contributed to the development of *lean production* techniques of manufacturing.

■ *e.g.* Henry Ford was the first manufacturer to use mass production on a large scale.

matrix management: approach to management in which teams of employees with appropriate skills are assembled to carry out particular tasks.

■ This style of management operates within an *organisational structure* of flexible teams, allowing individuals to use their skills to best effect. Project managers bring teams together for a relatively short time until the task is complete. Individuals might be part of two or more teams simultaneously.

■ *e.g.* Matrix management is used in businesses such as marketing agencies that manage a number of projects at one time.

Mayo, Elton: psychologist and founder of the *human relations* school of management.

■ Mayo was born in Adelaide, Australia. He lectured in ethics and psychology in Australia before emigrating to the USA, where he taught at Harvard Business School. He is best remembered for his experimental studies at Western Electric's Hawthorne plant, which suggested that labour productivity depended on workers' morale and that morale could be affected by social interaction in the workplace. Mayo's major theories are contained in *The Human Problems of an Industrial Civilization* (1933). See also *Hawthorne effect.*

MBO: see *management by objectives.*

mean (arithmetic): a single figure representing a group of data, calculated by adding all the numbers in the group together and dividing this total by the number of items in the group.

■ In effect, this is the *average*. It is a common method of finding a number representing a range of values.

Memorandum of Association: document containing details of a company's purpose in trading, the amount of capital it intends to raise and its registered name and address.

■ The Memorandum of Association is completed in conjunction with the *Articles of Association* and sent to the *Registrar of Companies* as part of the procedure necessary to establish a *company*. The Registrar of Companies holds a copy of the Memorandum of Association for every company at Companies House.

merchandising: series of techniques used by manufacturers to ensure that retailers sell the highest possible volume of their products.

■ Manufacturers use merchandising to achieve the best locations for their products in stores and to ensure that sufficient supplies (and extra outlets) are available for periods of peak demand. Merchandising is an aspect of *sales promotion* and is designed to appeal to retailers and consumers and to give a short-term boost to sales.

■ *e.g.* competitions, free samples, 'two for the price of one' offers and demonstrations of products.

merger: bringing together of two or more businesses to form a new enterprise.

■ A prime reason for mergers between rival businesses (*horizontal integration*) is to achieve *economies of scale*, allowing the newly formed business to be more competitive. Mergers also take place between firms in the same industry but at different stages of production (*vertical integration*): for example, a computer manufacturer joining with an electrical retailer. Finally, conglomerate mergers are a means of spreading risk by producing a diverse range of products. See also *integration*.

 e.g. Many high-profile mergers have taken place in the UK, such as the merging of the Halifax and Leeds Building Societies.

'me too' product: 'copycat' product introduced by a business following the success of a similar good or service supplied by another firm.

 It is not unusual for 'me too' products to be sold by supermarkets under their own brand label. Firms producing such products can avoid heavy expenditure on scientific and market research.

 e.g. Procter & Gamble introduced Febreze, a clothing and fabric deodorant spray; the product was instantly reproduced by dozens of imitators, which often sell their version at much lower prices.

 TIP Although 'me too' products are common in most industries, firms are limited in their ability to produce copycat products by *patents* and *copyright*.

microeconomics: study of problems and choices facing small units within the economy, such as the individual person, firm or industry.

 Microeconomics encompasses the study of why consumers take purchasing decisions, the setting of prices within a market and the implications for firms and consumers of particular *market structures*. See also *macroeconomics*.

minimum wage: lowest hourly rate an employer may legally pay.

 The UK government introduced a minimum wage on 1 April 1999. The main elements of the new legislation were: a general minimum wage rate of £3.60 per hour (raised to £3.70 in 2000); a minimum rate of £3 an hour (raised to £3.25) for all 18–21-year-olds; those on *piece-rate pay* and people employed on a part-time or temporary basis were to receive the minimum wage. Employers argued that having to pay more under the minimum wage legislation would result in the loss of thousands of jobs. In the event, their fears were unfounded and levels of employment have been maintained.

mission statement: brief outline of the general purpose of a business.

 Mission statements aim to provide a sense of direction to all employees in an organisation. For this reason they tend to be relatively brief. An organisation can derive its *corporate objectives* from its mission statement: by achieving these objectives, it should fulfil the business's mission statement.

 e.g. Microsoft's mission statement (adopted in 1999) is to 'empower people through great software any time, any place and in any device'.

mixed economy: economy containing elements of private enterprise and government involvement in production.

 All economies in the world are really mixed economies, with elements of both state and private enterprise; it is just the proportions that vary. One extreme of a mixed economy is Singapore, which comprises mainly private enterprise and little control by the government. On the other hand, the Chinese economy has a limited amount of private enterprise in a mainly state-controlled system. See also *market economy*.

monetary policy: attempt by governments (or central banks acting on their behalf) to manipulate the amount of money and interest rates in the economy in order to achieve the desired level of economic activity.

■ The two main elements of monetary policy are controlling the supply of money and adjusting the *interest rate*. The authorities attempt to control the money supply through influencing the level of lending by banks and through their own spending. Since 1997, the Monetary Policy Committee at the *Bank of England* has set the interest rate monthly.

■ *TIP* Successive governments have experienced great difficulty in controlling the supply of money. Because of this, recent governments have relied heavily on interest rates to control the level of economic activity.

monopolies and mergers legislation: series of Acts of Parliament intended to promote free and fair competition in UK markets.

■ This legislation is intended to avoid the exploitation of consumers and to encourage the development of new businesses by providing an environment in which they can flourish. The *Office of Fair Trading* and the *Competition Commission* oversee monopolies and mergers legislation in the UK.

■ *TIP* Remember when discussing monopolies and mergers legislation that the activities of UK businesses are increasingly influenced by EU rules on *monopolies* and *mergers*. If a conflict exists between UK and EU legislation on competition, the European laws take precedence.

monopoly: theoretical situation in which a single producer supplies a particular market.

■ The term is also used when a group of producers acts as a single producer through mutual agreement. In the UK, monopolies are not necessarily banned; action is taken against them only if they operate against the public interest by, for example, charging excessive prices. Monopolies can offer benefits to consumers by passing on the benefits of *economies of scale* in terms of lower prices and being able to afford research into new products. However, the *Competition Commission* can investigate any firm possessing a *market share* in excess of 25% if the circumstances warrant it.

mortgage: loan in which land or property is used as security.

■ If the individual or business arranging the mortgage fails to make repayments as promised, the financial institution lending the money can sell the property to recover its capital. Mortgages are long-term loans lasting for over 20 years. Because of the long-term nature of mortgages, they are usually subject to variable rates of interest. Mortgages are normally, but not always, used to provide funds with which to purchase property. See also *collateral*.

motivation: factors that influence people to behave in particular ways.

■ Some contend that motivation comes from inside employees and is therefore brought about by employees enjoying the task itself. Supporters of this view would advocate giving employees more complex and challenging tasks to motivate them. The alternative view is that motivation arises as a result of employees attempting to achieve goals or targets, perhaps in a monetary form. Supporters of this view would contend that money and production targets might be effective in motivating employees.

■ *TIP* The two ways of looking at motivation are very different and have important implications for the operation of organisations. If a manager believes that employees derive pleasure from fulfilling tasks, he or she is likely to offer employees substantial control over their working lives.

moving averages: a series of calculations designed to show the underlying *trend* in a series of data.

■ The use of moving averages should smooth out the impact of random variations in data and longer-term cyclical factors, thus highlighting the trend. Moving averages can be calculated over various periods of time, but a 3-year moving average is one of the most straightforward to calculate. See also *seasonal variation*.

■ *e.g.* In the following table, the annual bicycle sales for each of three successive years are added and the total is divided by three. The resulting figure is then plotted against the middle year of the three.

Annual sales of Marsh & Moore — bicycle manufacturers

Year	Bicycle sales	Three-year moving average
1991	1,500	—
1992	1,550	4,550 ÷ 3 = 1,517
1993	1,500	4,700 ÷ 3 = 1,567
1994	1,650	4,725 ÷ 3 = 1,575
1995	1,575	4,820 ÷ 3 = 1,607
1996	1,595	4,870 ÷ 3 = 1,623
1997	1,700	5,100 ÷ 3 = 1,700
1998	1,805	5,270 ÷ 3 = 1,757
1999	1,765	5,470 ÷ 3 = 1,823
2000	1,900	5,545 ÷ 3 = 1,848
2001	1,880	—

multinational: business with production capability in more than a single country.
■ Multinational companies operate a global strategy, making strategic decisions in terms of resources, facilities and markets available throughout the world. Many businesses trade as multinationals to exploit the cheap labour and other resources available in less developed countries. Furthermore, by selling in global markets, multinationals can reap the advantages of *economies of scale*. The trend in many markets is towards fewer, larger producers. For instance, there have been many *mergers* and *takeovers* in the car manufacturing industry in recent

years. Business analysts forecast that only three or four major producers will remain by 2015.

■ *e.g.* McDonald's, IBM and British American Tobacco.

■ *TIP* It is important to take a balanced view of multinationals. They have the potential to offer goods and services to global consumers at very low prices. On the other hand, multinationals have a reputation for unethical behaviour, paying pitifully low wages to employees in less developed countries and being responsible for damaging levels of pollution.

multiplier: the theory that changes in certain types of expenditure result in much greater changes in levels of income.

■ The multiplier predicts that increases in investment spending, government expenditure or purchases of exports by foreigners will result in the *national income* of the country rising by a greater amount. Similarly, reductions in these forms of expenditure will have a magnified downward effect on national income. The multiplier process is based on the principle that money entering the economy for the first time will be spent several times as it circulates, creating a greater final effect on income. John Maynard *Keynes* argued that governments should take this into account when managing the economy, so as to meet their economic objectives.

multi-skilling: giving employees the capability to fulfil a number of functions or roles in the organisation.

■ Giving employees a range of skills offers businesses a number of advantages. Employees can cover for absent colleagues, deal flexibly with sudden, unexpected increases in demand and might be more motivated by conducting a range of tasks. In these ways, a multi-skilled workforce can increase the competitiveness of a business and is essential for *lean production*. See also *job enlargement*.

mutual organisation: an enterprise that has no owners and is operated in the interests of the members of the organisation.

■ Mutual organisations aim to provide the highest quality service possible to their customers and any profits earned by the business are usually reinvested into the enterprise.

■ *e.g.* insurance companies, such as Standard Life, and building societies, such as the Buckinghamshire Building Society.

national income: total value of goods and services produced by an economy over a period of time, normally 1 year.

■ National income equals the value of an economy's total output because when individuals or organisations spend money on goods and services it represents the income of the business selling the good or service. The government uses *fiscal policy* and *monetary policy* to control the rate of growth of national income (and hence economic activity), in order to achieve its economic targets of price stability, low levels of unemployment and steady growth. See also *business cycle*.

nationalisation: transferring a privately owned organisation to the control of the state.

■ Nationalisation is regarded as an outdated policy by most governments. It is conventionally accepted that most industries operate more efficiently under private control and this has led to the denationalisation (or *privatisation*) of many industries. Most nationalisation in the UK took place in the 1940s and 1950s, but the majority of these industries have since been transferred back into private ownership.

natural wastage: decline in the size of a business's workforce as a result of employees leaving, retiring or dying.

■ Natural wastage depends upon management deciding not to replace these employees. It is allowed to happen when a firm wishes to reduce the size of its workforce and natural wastage might lessen or remove the need for *redundancy*.

negligence: when a person or an organisation fails to meet the standard of care expected and someone else suffers injury or loss as a consequence.

■ The duty of care relates to businesses in a number of ways. For example, firms have a duty of care to consumers to produce goods and services that are safe to use. Any person who suffers injury or loss as a result of negligence is entitled to take legal action to claim damages.

■ *TIP* Don't worry about the detail of legislation relating to businesses. It is sufficient to have a broad overview of the legislation and to appreciate the ways in which firms can be affected by their legal environment and how they might respond.

negotiation: process of bargaining through which two or more parties attempt to reach a mutually acceptable agreement.

■ Negotiation is commonplace in business. Firms negotiate with suppliers over prices and delivery dates; managers of a business negotiate among themselves over issues such as the launch date of a new product; *trade unions* and management negotiate over wages and working conditions. It is this last aspect of negotiation that attracts most attention. Effective negotiation requires experienced participants with particularly good communication skills, not least the ability to listen to the other side. Negotiation can be prolonged and complex and might require *arbitration* by a neutral third party to reach a successful conclusion.

net book value: current value of an *asset*, showing the original price paid for the item less any loss of value to date.

■ The value of a firm's assets is recorded on the *balance sheet* and their value is steadily written down over time through *depreciation*. The value of both *tangible* and *intangible assets* can be reduced over time and their annual worth recorded as net book value.

■ *e.g.* A firm might purchase a piece of machinery for £10 million and its value might be written down by £1 million each year. After 3 years the net book value of the machinery will be £7 million.

net cash flow: value of cash generated by a business compared with the expenditure of cash over the same period.

■ This is an important figure in a *cash-flow forecast*, indicating the monthly or annual cash position. An outflow of cash exceeding the inflow is termed a net outflow; the reverse is a net inflow. It is unlikely that a business could sustain a continual net outflow of cash. In these circumstances, it would be unable to settle its debts. It is a valuable part of financial planning to identify periods of net cash outflow, which will allow managers to make arrangements to cover the shortfall.

net current assets: see *working capital*.

net present value (NPV): value of the income generated by an investment, less its costs, expressed in terms of its current worth.

■ Future earnings are converted into their present-day values through discounting. This process uses the expected rate of interest as the basis for reducing the value of future earnings to represent their current worth. The longer the wait for income, the less it is worth in present-day terms. This is because a smaller amount could be invested and earn interest to equal the value of the future earnings. Net present value is a part of *discounted cash flow* techniques and is used by firms as a method of *investment appraisal*.

■ *TIP* It is important to appreciate the advantages of calculating the net present value of earnings by discounting. It allows businesses to compare the worth of two or more projects where income is received at different times. This permits better-quality investment decisions to be taken.

net profit: *sales revenue* of a business less all the costs incurred in production, including interest charges.

▓ Net profit can be expressed before or after tax has been paid on the profits. Net profit is a better indicator of a firm's performance than *gross profit* as all costs of production have been taken into account. See also *net profit margin*.

▓ **TIP** It is important to recognise that several forms of profit exist and to try to use terms such as 'net profit' precisely, rather than generally referring to 'profits'.

net profit margin: ratio expressing a firm's profit after the deduction of all costs as a percentage of income from sales or *turnover*.

▓ This ratio is calculated as follows:

$$\text{net profit margin} = \frac{\text{net profit}}{\text{turnover}} \times 100$$

In general, managers seek to achieve the highest possible net profit margin. The ratio gives some indication of the ability of the business to control its costs, and particularly its *indirect costs*. If a firm's gross profit margin is unchanged while its net profit margin is worsening, it might be that indirect costs are rising significantly. See also *gross profit margin*.

▓ **TIP** It is worthwhile considering a business's net profit margin over a period of time to see whether it is improving or deteriorating. This can give some indication of the success of an enterprise.

net realisable value: value of an *asset* once any costs associated with its sale have been deducted.

▓ Firms operating the accounting principle of prudence would use net realisable value as the basis for valuing assets in their *balance sheet*.

▓ **e.g.** A business might own retail property with a market value of £10 million. However, legal fees resulting from the sale of the property plus estate agent's charges might amount to £1 million. In these circumstances, the net realisable value of the asset is £9 million.

network analysis: technique used to plan and control projects involving a series of tasks that might occur simultaneously.

▓ Network analysis shows the quickest and most efficient means of completing complex tasks. It avoids unnecessary delays and assists in keeping costs as low as possible. See also *critical path analysis*.

New Deal: programme designed to give additional support to the long-term unemployed with the aim of returning them to work.

▓ New Deal offers help in getting a job through advice, support, quality training and work experience for those who have been unemployed for 6 months or more. New Deal's aim is to find unsubsidised jobs for people. If they are unsuccessful in this search, New Deal candidates can take a temporary job, undertake voluntary work or enter full-time education or training. Under any New Deal option, at least 1 day a week must be spent training to improve job skills.

New Deal was introduced by the Labour government in 1997 and was intended for unemployed people aged 18–25, but this age range was later extended.

newly industrialised country (NIC): a nation that has recently experienced the development of its economy and the rapid expansion of its manufacturing capability.

▓ This process is characterised by the decreasing dependence of the economy on agriculture and mineral extraction, and the creation of mass employment in manufacturing industry.

▓ *e.g.* Indonesia and Brazil.

NIC: see *newly industrialised country.*

niche market: relatively small and identifiable segment of a larger market.

▓ Niche markets can be very attractive to small firms, as they are often overlooked by large businesses and are therefore less competitive. Firms selling in niche markets can also sometimes charge high prices. However, selling in a niche market can be risky: for example, demand for products in such markets often declines significantly during an economic *recession*. See also *mass markets.*

▓ *e.g.* The demand for alcohol-free beers and wines is a niche market and part of the wider wines and spirits market.

▓ *TIP* This is a very common area for questions, especially those asking candidates to compare the behaviour of businesses in niche and mass markets.

nominal capital: see *authorised share capital.*

non-executive director: director of a company who is not primarily employed by the business.

▓ Non-executive directors do not play a part in the day-to-day management of the business, and are likely to be employed by other businesses or organisations. Non-executive directors bring a particular specialism to a business, making their major contribution at meetings of *boards of directors.* Members of Parliament are often non-executive directors, supplying an insight into the political environment in which a business trades.

non-price competition: range of techniques used by businesses to increase sales and market share without using price.

▓ This form of competition is common between *oligopolies* that fear the uncertainty that might result from a *price war.* It is used extensively by petrol retailers: for example, in the increasing range of forecourt services.

▓ *e.g.* advertising, loyalty cards, gifts, competitions and other promotions.

non-profit-making organisation: any enterprise that seeks objectives other than profits.

▓ Non-profit-making organisations might pursue objectives such as protecting the community or providing the best possible service to their members. Any surpluses earned by these organisations are usually put back into the business for the benefit of those receiving their goods or services.

▓ *e.g.* the police, schools and colleges, hospitals and, most notably, mutual organisations such as insurance companies and building societies.

normal distribution: frequency distribution for data that has a symmetrical bell-shape.

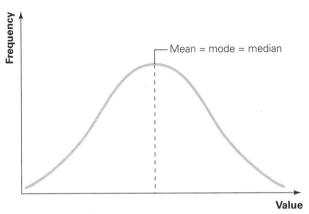

- Many data related to businesses, if collected in sufficient quantities, tend to have a normal distribution. A normal distribution has the unusual property that its mode, mean and median all have the same value.
- *e.g.* It is commonly assumed that the IQ of the UK's population is normally distributed around an *average* or mean of 100.

no-strike agreement: accord between an employer and the representatives of the workforce that they will not take strike action for some specified period.

- This type of arrangement is an aspect of *Japanisation* that has spread to firms in many western countries. It requires employers to treat employees favourably and that both sides accept *binding arbitration* should a dispute occur.

NPV: see *net present value.*

objectives: targets or goals pursued by an enterprise that shape the policies it implements.

■ The precise objectives of any business will depend upon the aspirations of its owners, the strength and actions of its competitors and the financial position of the business. Businesses have a hierarchy of objectives as illustrated in the diagram below. See also *corporate objectives* and *mission statement*.

■ *e.g.* The major objectives of commercial organisations are survival, profit and growth. *Non-profit-making organisations* might have different aims, such as providing a service to their members.

obsolescence: when a product is no longer in demand, having reached the end of its *product life cycle*.

■ Obsolescence might occur because newer products exist based on more advanced technology, or because tastes and fashions change. In certain markets, scientific or *market research* is essential to counter the threat of obsolescence. However, it also offers opportunities for firms to introduce new products.

■ *e.g.* Much computer technology becomes obsolete fairly quickly; fashion clothes fall out of favour as tastes and designs change.

Office of Fair Trading (OFT): government organisation, established in 1973, with broad responsibilities for ensuring free and fair competition and consumer protection.

■ The OFT is led by the Director-General of Fair Trading (DGFT). Its Competition Policy Division promotes effective competition in UK markets, improving the competitiveness of UK businesses. The division removes or limits restrictions on competition as well as improving the effectiveness of competition law. The Consumer Affairs Division monitors the markets for goods and services in order to analyse trends and identify potential problem areas. It is responsible for the OFT's advice to the government on consumer policy issues. An important aspect of this work is providing advice on EU consumer policy proposals.

off-the-job training: provision of job-related skills and knowledge outside the workplace (e.g. at a local college).

▓ Off-the-job training can take the form of external courses, perhaps including lectures or seminars. A significant number of training organisations supply off-the-job training in the form of distance learning or self-study, which takes place mainly at the employee's home. This form of off-the-job training is relatively cheap and employees can fit it in around their other commitments. Firms supplying this type of training make extensive use of the Internet and other forms of communications technology. See also *training* and *on-the-job training*.

OFT: see *Office of Fair Trading*.

ogive: line graph showing the cumulative frequency of a given distribution of data.

▓ Ogives present data in the form of a running total with each class in the data added to the one above to give a frequency figure that builds up cumulatively.

▓ *e.g.* The following diagram shows how to derive an ogive from the marks of a group of students in a business studies examination.

Marks in the examination	Number of candidates
30–39	25
40–49	31
50–59	42
60–69	29
70–79	18

These data can be rearranged as follows:

Marks		Cumulative frequency
Under 40		25
Under 50	(25 + 31)	56
Under 60	(25 + 31 + 42)	98
Under 70	(25 + 31 + 42 + 29)	127
Under 80	(25 + 31 + 42 + 29 + 18)	145

They can then be plotted on an ogive as shown:

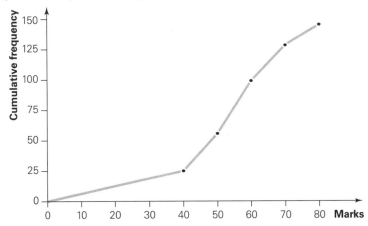

oligopoly: market in which a few firms control most of the output of a particular good or service.

▧ In an oligopolistic market, each firm considers the likely response of its rivals to any action before implementing it. Thus, an oligopolist would consider the possible reactions of other firms in the market before introducing a new product or commencing a major advertising campaign. Oligopolists traditionally avoid price competition for fear of price wars. Some oligopolists practise *collusion* to keep prices high or to agree standards for their products.

▧ *e.g.* Mobile telephone services are sold in an oligopolistic market with only a few sellers, such as Orange and Vodafone.

ombudsman: person or organisation that aims to resolve disputes between consumers and suppliers in certain markets.

▧ Ombudsmen are individuals supported by administrative staff who deal with complaints from consumers dissatisfied with the standard of good or service provided. They perform a particularly important role where there is only a single supplier of a service (e.g. local government) and where the competitive spur to quality provision is absent. Some commercial ombudsman schemes are compulsory; others can only request firms to be a part of the system.

▧ *e.g.* The National Health Service, local governments, the banking industry and estate agents all operate ombudsmen.

one-way communication: process by which information and ideas are passed down a hierarchy with no response permitted.

▧ This form of *communication* is most likely in an autocratic organisation such as the army or the emergency services. Such communication ensures that leaders retain control of an organisation, but might make it unresponsive and might not result in the most effective use of employees.

on-line trading see *e-commerce*.

on-the-job training: provision of job-related skills and knowledge at the place of work.

▧ This form of training often requires employees to learn from more experienced workers through observation or work shadowing. Alternatively, the trainee might work through instruction manuals, operate with a mentor or receive more formal guidance from senior employees. See also *training* and *off-the-job training*.

operating profit (also called 'trading profit'): surplus arising from a business's normal trading activities.

▧ Operating profit is calculated by subtracting *overheads* or *indirect costs* (e.g. depreciation or the wages paid to administrative staff) from *gross profit*. Operating profit excludes any income that the business might receive from non-trading activities (e.g. dividends on shares in other companies or rent from properties that are leased out). Operating profit is recorded on the *profit and loss account*. See also *profit*.

▧ *TIP* It is important to recognise that several forms of profit exist. Try to use terms such as 'operating profit' precisely, rather then generally referring to 'profits'.

opportunity cost: cost of using resources expressed in terms of the best alternative use.

■ Opportunity cost is a concept used by economists seeking the most effective use of resources and it does not place a monetary value on these resources. Every decision relating to resources has an opportunity cost, as all resources can be used in more than one way.

■ *e.g.* A firm might choose to use a derelict brewery to produce soft drinks for children. The opportunity cost of this decision might be redeveloping the factory space into an industrial museum.

oral communication: see *verbal communication*.

ordinary share (also called 'equity share'): a financial security representing the ownership of part of a limited company.

■ Ordinary shares are the most common type of *share* and are issued by most companies. They carry a high level of risk because the *dividends* paid to the holders of such shares are entirely dependent upon the profitability of the business. There is no fixed payment. Because of this degree of risk, holders of ordinary shares are entitled to vote at company meetings.

■ *TIP* Some companies issue non-voting ordinary shares so that they can raise more capital while allowing the existing *shareholders* to retain control of the business.

organisational structure: how roles in a particular enterprise are arranged to allow it to perform its activities.

■ A business's structure establishes the relationships between the different components of the organisation, including its lines of communication and authority. Organisational structures can be 'tall' or 'flat' depending upon the number of *levels of hierarchy* and the *spans of control* operated by managers.

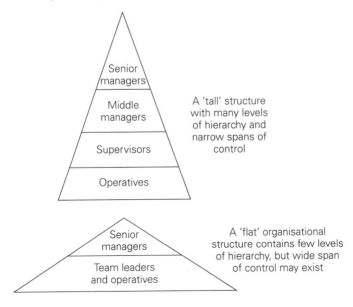

It has become increasingly common for organisations to flatten their structures, to reduce wage costs and empower shop-floor workers. See also *delayering*.

overcapacity: see *excess capacity*.

overdraft: flexible loan on which an individual or business can draw without notice up to some agreed limit.

Overdrafts are flexible: firms only pay for what they borrow and can use the facility whenever they want. They are simple and quick to arrange, but can be expensive. Interest is often charged at between 4% and 6% over a bank's normal lending rate. Overdrafts are negotiated between banks and businesses for some agreed period, and the amount depends upon the firm's financial history and earning capacity.

TIP An overdraft is a short-term method of finance. As it is expensive, firms should seek to convert overdrafts to a cheaper source of finance, rather than use them in the long term.

overgeared: describes a company whose long-term borrowing exceeds 50% of its capital.

A company will normally aim to raise a maximum of 50% of its capital through borrowing. An overgeared firm represents a financial risk for *shareholders* — the company might be unable to pay satisfactory *dividends* if its profits fall, as it has a heavy commitment to pay interest charges on its loans. Overgeared firms might also be vulnerable to increases in *interest rates*. See also *gearing*.

overheads: expenses that are not related to a particular product or aspect of the business's activities.

Overheads are *indirect costs* such as office or factory rents, wages of administrative staff, costs of running a sales team and expenditure on maintenance and security. Those departments in a business that supply services to all parts of the organisation normally generate overheads. Some firms attempt to divide up their overheads among the various products sold by the business through the process of *absorption costing*; others rely on *contribution costing*, which avoids the need to allocate overheads.

overtime: hours worked in excess of an agreed number per day or week.

Employees usually receive a higher rate of pay for working overtime hours, often expressed as a proportion of the standard hourly rate. Paying workers overtime allows firms to respond flexibly to changing patterns of demand without the expense and difficulty of recruiting extra staff. It also lessens the chance of idle workers or *redundancy* if the business encounters a slack period.

e.g. Employees working overtime (for example, on a Sunday) might receive time-and-a-half: that is, 50% more than their usual hourly rate.

overtrading: where a business expands too rapidly without arranging funds to finance its growth.

A period of rapid growth will commit a business to increased expenditure on labour, materials and fuel to produce the additional goods or services. However, the firm might have to wait some time before receiving payment from its customers. This problem is exacerbated if businesses have to offer *trade credit* to attract new customers. If this occurs over a prolonged period, a business might encounter severe *liquidity* problems and be unable to pay suppliers or employees.

own-brand product: a good sold by retailers that carries the retailer's own name.

■ Own-brand goods are normally cheaper than those bearing the name of a manufacturer, although some retailers have created more exclusive own-brand products. These products have seen a substantial rise in popularity over the last 20 years, partly because retailers earn a larger profit margin on them. Own-brand products are most commonly found in supermarkets and clothing stores.

■ *e.g.* Many large retailers, such as Marks & Spencer and Tesco, stock a wide range of own-brand products.

Pacific rim countries: countries that have a coastline on to the Pacific Ocean.

■ Some business analysts argue that these countries are likely to enjoy very high rates of growth during the early years of the twenty-first century and might become increasingly influential in the global economy. They are sometimes considered as an economic grouping.

■ *e.g.* Japan, South Korea and Australia.

packaging: wrapping of goods for the purposes of protection and *promotion*.

■ Packaging is particularly important for products where consumers take purchasing decisions at the *point-of-sale* (e.g. confectionery). Consumers purchasing such products are frequently influenced in their choice by the colours and materials used to package products. In recent years, packaging has become more sophisticated, providing a secure environment for products, but also increasing costs. Some businesses have sought competitive advantage by highlighting their use of environmentally-friendly packaging. In the 1990s, UK businesses spent nearly as much on packaging as on promotion.

■ *TIP* Some textbooks include packaging in the *marketing mix*, making the 5Ps. It is more usual, however, for packaging to be included within promotion.

parallel imports: goods brought into a country by an enterprise working on its own rather than as official distributor for the manufacturer.

■ Parallel imports occur when firms practise *price discrimination*. They are expected to increase if the UK adopts the euro, as consumers will be able to compare prices more easily and will seek alternative and cheaper sources of supply.

■ *e.g.* Small UK distributors are purchasing top-brand motorcycles in the Netherlands (where they are much cheaper than in the UK) and reselling them in the UK at a substantial profit. This limits the opportunities for companies such as Honda to maximise profits by charging different prices in different markets. See also *grey market*.

participative leadership: see *democratic leadership*.

partnership: group of between 2 and 20 people who contribute finance and expertise to an enterprise.

■ The deed of partnership details the amount of capital that partners have contributed and how profits are to be shared, as well as arrangements for dissolving the business. The legal rules under which partnerships are established are set out in the Partnership Act 1890. Forming a partnership offers the opportunity to bring in specialist skills (e.g. a solicitor experienced in family law into a law firm) as well as sharing the pressures of managing a business. Partners do not generally benefit from *limited liability*, although unlimited partnerships are possible, where partners who are just investing capital, but not playing a part in the business, do benefit from limited liability.

■ *e.g.* Partnerships are common in the professions, such as solicitors, estate agents and doctors.

■ *TIP* The most important aspect of partnership to know is its advantages and disadvantages in relation to other forms of business structure.

patent: document granting an individual or business the sole right to benefit from an invention for a specified period.

■ Patents give their holders the right to make and sell a product, thereby preventing others from copying it, for periods of up to 20 years. They are widely used in industries such as pharmaceuticals and computer software. Enterprises can gain patents effective in the UK, Europe or throughout the world. Patents in the UK are administered by the Patents Office and are legally enforceable under the Copyright, Designs and Patents Act 1988.

paternalistic leadership: style in which leaders take decisions in what they consider to be the best interests of their employees.

■ Paternalistic leaders tend to explain their decisions to their subordinates and might engage in some limited use of *delegation*. *Communication* under paternalistic leaders is normally downward only. They tend to look after the social and sporting needs of their employees, providing good facilities for staff. *Trade unions* often oppose paternalistic leadership as they seek to allow their members to operate more independently.

payback: technique of investment appraisal that evaluates individual projects in terms of the time taken to recover the original outlay.

■ Payback allows managers to assess the value of a project or to rank a number of products in order of desirability. It has the advantage of being relatively simple to calculate, but it ignores the overall profitability of investment projects. See also *investment appraisal*.

■ *e.g.* In the following example, project A achieves payback in 3 years and project B in 2 years.

| | Cash flows (£) | |
	Project A	Project B
Initial investment	(25,000)	(10,000)
Cash inflow, year 1	8,000	6,000
Cash inflow, year 2	8,000	4,000
Cash inflow, year 3	9,000	2,000
Cash inflow, year 4	9,000	1,000

P/E: see *price–earnings ratio.*

pendulum arbitration: using a third party to settle a dispute by selecting the complete case of one side or the other.

■ This form of arbitration avoids the situation where arbitrators seek a compromise settlement. It avoids parties to a dispute adopting extreme positions in negotiations, as this would result in the other side's case being chosen. Pendulum arbitration is a form of *binding arbitration,* meaning that both parties to the dispute agree to accept the decision at the outset of the process. See also *arbitration.*

penetration pricing: pricing strategy under which a firm sets a price below the current market price with the aim of increasing sales.

■ Firms entering a market frequently use this strategy to build up *market share* as quickly as possible. They increase their volume of sales, but earn a lower profit on each sale. Once the business has achieved its target market share, it might increase price with the aim of maximising long-term profits. However, penetration pricing is risky, as it might lead to rivals lowering prices as a competitive response or consumers perceiving the product as low quality.

■ *TIP* Pricing involves strategy and method. Penetration pricing is a *pricing strategy* — that is, a general approach. *Pricing methods* are ways in which firms determine the exact price — for example, based on the costs of production.

perfect competition: theoretical model of 'pure' competition within a market, in which many small businesses compete on an equal basis.

■ This model assumes that firms have equal and complete access to knowledge about the market, produce identical products and can enter and leave the markets freely. Such criteria are expected to result in the most intense competition possible, offering consumers the lowest possible prices.

■ *TIP* This is a theoretical model that does not exist in real life. You should not learn too much of the theory, but simply use the concept as a yardstick against which the degree of competition within a real market can be assessed.

performance indicators (PIs): series of measures used to assess the achievement of individuals and organisations in the business world.

■ Individuals might be assessed against PIs as part of their *appraisal.* In these circumstances, relevant indicators might include sales figures or levels of labour productivity. Organisations might face PIs such as *market share* and measures of customer satisfaction. Performance indicators have increased in popularity as the use of target setting (especially in the public sector) has become more widespread. See also *performance-related pay.*

performance-related pay (PRP): system of rewarding employees that is linked to the attainment of some agreed targets.

■ Under PRP, employees might receive a pay increase only if they achieve a particular level of sales, win a certain number of new customers or keep costs within a given level. More sophisticated systems operate on a scale, with varying rates of pay increase dependent upon the exact performance of the employee. PRP is normally an integral part of an enterprise's *appraisal* system. Its popularity has declined a little in recent years as firms have sought less controversial systems.

■ *e.g.* The National Health Service and financial institutions such as banks make extensive use of PRP.

peripheral workers: employees hired on a part-time or temporary basis, often with relatively few skills and receiving commensurately low rates of pay.

■ Peripheral workers are usually on the fringes of an organisation's workforce and allow it to respond flexibly to changes in market conditions. This type of employee is normally used alongside full-time salaried and skilled employees, known as 'core workers'. See also *flexible working*.

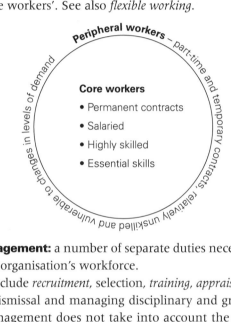

personnel management: a number of separate duties necessary for the administration of an organisation's workforce.

■ These duties include *recruitment*, selection, *training*, *appraisal*, payment of *wages* and *salaries*, dismissal and managing disciplinary and grievance procedures. Personnel management does not take into account the integration of these activities in pursuit of *corporate objectives*; instead these tasks are viewed as discrete. Hence the philosophy of personnel management does not elevate managing the organisation's human resources to the level of a strategic issue to be considered by senior managers. See also *human resource management*.

person specification: see *job specification*.

persuasive advertising: communicating with potential customers to encourage them to purchase a particular good or service.

■ This form of *advertising* is more common than *informative advertising* and is often used to convince consumers to purchase a particular product rather than that produced by a rival enterprise. If used repeatedly, it might also build up *brand loyalty* and increase *market share*. This form of advertising has been criticised on ethical grounds for creating a desire for products that did not previously exist and for targeting vulnerable groups in society (e.g. children and those addicted to tobacco).

PEST analysis: method of assessing the likely impact of the political, economic, social and technological factors in the external environment of a business.

- Through categorising these external factors, a business can analyse the constraints they might have on the enterprise and allow managers to put together a coherent strategy to deal with them.

- *TIP* Some textbooks use the acronym SLEPT (social, legal, economic, political and technical) to perform similar analyses of the external environment in which an organisation operates.

Peters, Tom: author and lecturer on business and management.

- Peters was born in Baltimore, in the USA, in 1942. He was a management consultant before founding the Tom Peters Group. His bestseller (written with Robert Waterman), *In Search of Excellence* (1982), analysed successful business practices and became a business bible. The book focuses on the benefits to management of doing simple things uncommonly well and the importance of *organisational structure* to business success. Peters developed these themes in *Thriving on Chaos* (1989) and *A Passion for Excellence* (1992).

picketing: attempt by those involved in an *industrial dispute* to prevent others from entering the place of work.

- By persuasion and, in some cases, intimidation, workers involved in an industrial dispute use picketing to try to prevent non-union workers, employees who are ignoring the action, or members of other *trade unions* from going to work. Legislation introduced in the 1980s has limited the effectiveness of picketing. For example, the number of workers allowed on picket lines has been restricted and workers are not permitted to picket any place at which they do not work (secondary picketing).

piece-rate pay (also called 'piecework'): system whereby workers are paid per unit of output produced.

- Piece-rate pay is common in agriculture (e.g. fruit-picking) and the textile industry (e.g. home knitters are paid for each garment they produce). Although using a piece-rate pay system helps to control costs, it discourages high-quality products, as employees are encouraged to work as quickly as possible. The implementation of the national *minimum wage* has made piece-rate pay more difficult to operate as employees have to receive at least the minimum wage.

piecework: see *piece-rate pay.*

PIs: see *performance indicators.*

place: see *distribution.*

plc: see *public limited company.*

ploughed-back profit: see *retained profit.*

point-of-sale: location at which a consumer makes a purchasing decision.

- In most cases, the point-of-sale is a shop or other retail outlet. An increasing proportion of purchases (e.g. confectionery, furniture, food products) results from in-store decisions, so point-of-sale promotional material is of growing importance.

e.g. window displays, display racks, self-service cartons and *packaging*. Some manufacturers use 'sniff teasers', which give off a pleasant aroma representing the product.

PR: see *public relations*.

predatory pricing (also called 'destroyer pricing'): establishing a price below the current market price with the intention of eliminating other, less efficient businesses.

This is a highly aggressive policy designed to increase sales and *market share*, but one that is unlikely to be maintained in the long run. It is also a risky strategy, as it reduces a firm's *profit margin* and might result in a *price war*, the outcome of which is likely to be uncertain.

e.g. The airline industry has seen a number of cases of predatory pricing by, for example, British Airways.

TIP Pricing involves strategy and method. Predatory pricing is a *pricing strategy* — that is, a general approach. *Pricing methods* are ways in which firms determine the exact price — for example, based on the costs of production.

preference share: special type of financial security representing the ownership of part of a limited company.

Preference *shareholders* receive their share of profits before any payment is made to holders of *ordinary shares*. If the company earns low profits, there might only be sufficient to pay preference shareholders. Because preference shareholders bear less risk, they receive only a fixed rate of return (e.g. 6% of the face value of the share) whatever the level of profits earned by the business. Some preference shares are cumulative, allowing shareholders' entitlements to profits to accumulate. Thus if the profits are insufficient to pay the fixed return in one year, the balance owing is carried forward to a more profitable period.

present value (PV): value of the income generated by an investment, expressed in terms of its current worth.

Future earnings are converted into their present-day values through the process of discounting. This process uses the expected rate of interest as the basis for reducing the value of future earnings to represent their current worth. The longer the wait for income, the less it is worth in present-day terms. This is because a smaller amount could be invested and earn interest to equal the value of the future earnings. See also *net present value* and *discounted cash flow*.

press release: brief business news items provided to the media for dissemination to their audiences.

Press releases are normally written, but might also be given orally at a press conference or via a telephone briefing. Press releases can be controlled by the organisation concerned and provide a cheap form of *promotion*. See also *public relations*.

pressure group: group of people with common interests who influence public opinion and the decisions of businesses and governments.

■ Pressure groups operate by lobbying. This might take the form of producing leaflets or organising demonstrations. In some circumstances, they might resort to direct action, such as occupying business premises to prevent firms taking certain actions, while drawing public attention to the issue.

■ *e.g.* Various types of pressure group exist. Cause or promotional pressure groups, such as Friends of the Earth and the Campaign for Nuclear Disarmament (CND), promote a distinct cause or issue. Interest groups, such as the Trades Union Congress and the Consumers' Association, promote and protect the interests of certain groups in society.

■ *TIP* It is important to relate the effects of pressure groups to the business or businesses in question. Some businesses (e.g. those with potential to pollute or those in highly competitive markets) are especially susceptible to the actions of pressure groups.

price discrimination: charging separate groups of customers different prices for the same good or service.

■ Through price discrimination, businesses aim to charge a higher price to consumers whose demand is more price inelastic. Simultaneously, they offer a lower price to customers with more price-elastic demand. In this way, the company benefits from having large numbers of customers as well as charging those for whom the product is essential a high price. Profits are increased as a result. For price discrimination to work effectively, businesses must be able to separate the various groups of consumers.

■ *e.g.* Commuters pay higher rail fares than those travelling at other times. Those using telephone services in the evening and at weekends pay lower call charges.

price–earnings (P/E) ratio: measure of a company's position in the market calculated by dividing the company's share price by its earnings per share.

$$P/E \text{ ratio} = \frac{\text{market price of ordinary shares}}{\text{earnings per share}}$$

The 'market price of ordinary shares' is simply the current price at which the *ordinary shares* of the company are traded. 'Earnings per share' are calculated by dividing profit on ordinary trading activities after tax by the number of ordinary shares issued. Thus if a company's profit amounted to £1 per share and the market price of its shares was £12, the P/E ratio would be 12. In general, a higher figure is preferable as it reflects more confidence in the business's future. An average P/E ratio might be about 12, with the ratio of a stable *blue-chip company* at around 15, and that for a high-profile company achieving rapid growth at about 20. Key factors influencing the value of a company's P/E ratio are its track record, the view investors hold of its future and the type of industry in which the firm operates.

price elasticity of demand: sensitivity of demand for a product to changes in its price.

■ This is an important theoretical concept within business studies. Price elasticity of demand is measured by the following formula:

$$\text{price elasticity of demand} = \frac{\% \text{ change in quantity demanded}}{\% \text{ change in price}}$$

Demand for a good is said to be price elastic if it is highly sensitive to price changes. With elastic goods, a given percentage change in price provokes a larger percentage change in demand (e.g. a 10% rise in price leads to a 20% fall in demand). When demand is price elastic, the formula will produce an answer greater than 1 (in this case, 20/10 = 2). In contrast, demand for a good is described as price inelastic when it is not sensitive to price changes. With inelastic goods, a given percentage change in price results in a smaller percentage change in demand (e.g. a 10% fall in price leads to a 5% increase in demand). When demand is price inelastic, the formula will produce an answer less than 1 (in this case, 5/10 = 0.5).

price fixing: setting of prices by governments or businesses, rather than by market forces.

▨ Governments might set prices to prevent undesirable price competition (e.g. the price of MOT tests for motorcars). Firms might collude to set prices at a level designed to generate high profits and exploit consumers. Such *collusion* will limit demand and in most cases is illegal.

price leader: firm in a particular market that announces major price changes, to be copied by other (often smaller) businesses.

▨ Price leadership is common in oligopolistic markets, where firms seek to avoid potentially damaging price competition. Where price leadership exists, businesses frequently compete through *promotion* and *product differentiation*. See also *oligopoly*.

▨ *e.g.* Levis is regarded as the price leader in the market for denims.

price skimming: pricing strategy under which a firm sets its prices high to attract the relatively small number of consumers whose demand is not sensitive to price.

▨ Price skimming ('skimming the cream' of the market) is commonly used when firms launch new products, and especially technologically sophisticated products. Skimming offers businesses the chance to establish a reputation for a quality product, providing a sound basis for selling later to a *mass market*. Simultaneously, skimming provides a high *profit margin* on each sale and assists firms in recouping research costs. See also *penetration pricing*.

▨ *e.g.* Initially, mobile telephones were aimed at the business community, which was able and willing to pay high prices for a new product.

▨ *TIP* Pricing involves strategy and method. Price skimming is a *pricing strategy* — that is, a general approach. *Pricing methods* are ways in which firms determine the exact price — for example, based on the costs of production.

price taker: firm that sets a price equal to the 'going rate' or established *market price*.

■ Price takers have no influence over the market price, as they are one of many small firms competing for business. Because their products are similar, an increase in price will result in a heavy loss of sales. Price takers exist in the model of *perfect competition*, but they are not common in the real economy.

■ *e.g.* market gardeners growing fruit and vegetables.

price transparency: situation in which consumers can easily compare the prices of products supplied by rival businesses.

■ Price transparency might occur because firms offer products in similar quantities, with similar 'extras' or the same after-sales service, e.g. air travel. One of the arguments for the UK adopting the European single currency (the euro) is that it will be easy for consumers (individuals and businesses) to compare the prices of products from all parts of the EU without the confusion of different currencies and changing *exchange rates*.

price war: period of aggressive price cuts by competitors in a particular market seeking to increase their *market share*.

■ In most circumstances, firms avoid price wars because they reduce the profits of all the businesses concerned and there are no real 'winners'. The fear of price wars has resulted in firms competing in other ways (e.g. *promotion* and *product differentiation*). See also *oligopoly*.

■ *e.g.* The national newspaper market has seen sporadic price wars, with *The Times* selling for as little as 10p.

■ *TIP* Firms are reluctant to engage in price wars because they are happiest taking decisions where the outcomes are reasonably certain. The less certain the outcome of a decision (as in the case of a price war), the less likely firms will be to take it.

pricing method: way in which a firm calculates its selling price.

■ Businesses tend to calculate their price by taking into account one or more of the following: the costs of production; the price that consumers will be willing to pay; and prices charged by rival firms. Firms might rely on one of these factors or use a combination of them. Thus a firm might calculate its cost of production for a particular good and add on a *mark-up* for profit, but recognising that this will make it more expensive than rivals' products, it might then lower its price a little to reflect market conditions.

pricing strategy: philosophy underpinning the pricing decisions taken by a business.

■ Pricing strategy is an important part of the overall *marketing strategy*. A number of pricing strategies are open to businesses. For existing products: prestige pricing, designed to reinforce a quality image; acting as the *price leader*, where the business is the major firm in the market; and acting as a *price taker*, where it accepts the going *market price*. For new products: *price skimming*, where the firm sets the price high to catch those consumers willing to pay top prices; and *penetration pricing*, where it sets the price low to increase *market share*.

pricing tactics: series of pricing techniques that are normally used only over the short term to achieve specific goals.

- The aim of pricing tactics is usually to produce a short-term increase in sales, perhaps in response to a competitor launching a new product or reducing prices.
- *e.g.* *loss leaders* and special offers such as 'buy two, get one free'.
- *TIP* It is important to understand the difference between *pricing strategies, pricing methods* and pricing tactics, and to use these terms effectively when answering examination questions.

primary data: information collected directly from potential customers by asking questions or observing behaviour.

- Primary data are generally more time consuming and costly to collect than *secondary data*. However, they can provide more up-to-date and relevant information, enabling firms to take more informed decisions. See also *primary research*.
- *e.g.* Examples of primary data include the results of *questionnaires* and telephone surveys and interviews.

primary efficiency ratio: see *return on capital employed*.

primary research: gathering marketing information for the first time to meet a specific objective.

- Primary research could be undertaken into consumers' needs, market trends, competitors' products and prices, and the size of the market. It can be carried out in a number of ways. Many firms question potential customers using *questionnaires*, telephone or postal surveys, or interviews. Others choose to observe consumers making purchases or experiment with changing prices and products and analysing the outcomes. Primary research entails a fundamental trade-off between cost and accuracy. The greater the amount of information, the more expensive it will be to collect and analyse. See also *secondary research*.

primary sector: those industries involved in producing raw materials, fuels and other basic products.

- The primary sector includes agriculture, forestry, fishing, mining and quarrying. The importance of this sector as a contributor to a nation's *gross national product*, and in terms of employment, declines as an economy develops. See also *secondary sector* and *tertiary sector*.

private limited company (Ltd): relatively small company whose *shares* cannot be freely traded.

- Private limited companies are denoted by the letters 'Ltd' after the business's name. This indicates that *shareholders* purchasing company shares have the privilege of *limited liability*, restricting their financial commitment in the event of the business's *liquidation*. Private limited companies cannot sell their shares on the *Stock Exchange* and the permission of other shareholders has to be sought before shares can be sold. Private limited companies are not legally obliged to disclose as much financial information as *public limited companies*.

■ *e.g.* This type of company is very common and examples range from small family businesses to large, nationally known organisations such as the Virgin Group.

private sector: those businesses that are owned by individuals or other businesses.

■ This is in contrast to those business organisations owned by the state (the public sector). A major *corporate objective* of private sector organisations is to maximise profits.

■ *e.g.* *sole traders, partnerships, companies* and *cooperatives*.

privatisation: transferring organisations from state ownership to being owned and controlled by individuals and other businesses.

■ The arguments for privatisation include increasing the efficiency of the organisation and improving the quality of the product supplied to customers. The sale of state-owned industries through privatisation also raises large sums of money for the government, allowing tax cuts. The UK led the way in privatisation — a policy that has since been copied by governments across the globe. See also *nationalisation*.

■ *e.g.* In the 1980s and 1990s, many major state enterprises were sold into the *private sector*, including British Steel, British Coal, British Rail and the Water Boards.

probability: chance of a particular event occurring.

■ Businesses calculate probabilities in relation to a number of their activities. Thus they might calculate the probability of a particular product succeeding or of a specific marketing campaign achieving its objectives. Probability is an important element in some decision-making techniques (e.g. *decision trees*).

product design: planning a new good or service, deciding upon its features, functions and appearance.

■ Firms can gain a competitive advantage from selling well-designed products. *Market research* can play an important role in ensuring that the design of a product matches consumer requirements. It is also important that a product is designed so as to allow cost-effective production.

■ *e.g.* Jaguar and Sony have reputations for well-designed products, allowing them to charge premium prices.

product development: selling new or improved versions of products into existing markets.

■ Product development is an important strategy in the pharmaceutical industry, where many patented medicines have recently been offered in different forms (e.g. soluble and as lozenges). It is also important to firms in highly competitive markets, where a commercial advantage might be achieved by the regular introduction of new (and better) products. This might require businesses to invest heavily in *research and development* to generate new products and fuel the process of *innovation*. Product development is one of the strategies that can be analysed through *Ansoff's matrix*.

TIP Some firms regularly develop new *brands* in an attempt to 'crowd out' the opposition. Firms in the cigarette market use this technique extensively.

product differentiation: creation of a strong *brand* image through distinguishing a firm's products from those produced by competitors.

Product differentiation can assist a business in developing *brand loyalty* for its products and might make demand for the product more price inelastic, offering the firm a competitive advantage.

e.g. The Co-operative Bank has created product differentiation between the services it supplies and those supplied by other financial institutions by adopting an ethical stance. This has been at the heart of much of its subsequent marketing activity.

production: all activities involved in the transformation of inputs such as raw materials and labour services into saleable products.

Production takes a number of different forms, of which *mass production* is perhaps the most well known. However, a more recent approach is *lean production*.

TIP Production does not simply relate to goods achieved as a result of manufacturing. It is also the process by which services such as insurance and health care are supplied.

production line (also called 'assembly line'): manufacturing system whereby products move steadily along a conveyor belt while the process of production is completed.

A production line is appropriate for *mass production* involving large quantities of similar products. Operatives on a production line carry out a series of activities such as adding components and checking for quality. Production lines often require employees to complete simple and monotonous tasks repeatedly. Because of this, they have proved a difficult environment in which to motivate employees.

productivity: relationship between inputs into the production process and the resultant outputs.

Businesses commonly calculate labour productivity by dividing the output achieved over a period of time by the number of workers. Capital productivity relates to the output per machine per time period. Productivity is an important determinant of a business's competitiveness. High productivity levels give a business an edge in terms of costs.

e.g. If a factory produces 100,000 cars annually using 2,000 workers, the labour productivity of the enterprise is 50 cars per worker per year (100,000/2,000).

TIP Remember when answering examination questions that productivity does not only relate to the labour force. Capital productivity is important, especially in high-technology industries.

product life cycle: theory describing the stages that a product passes through during its existence in the marketplace.

■ The following diagram shows a typical product life cycle and its associated *cash flow*.

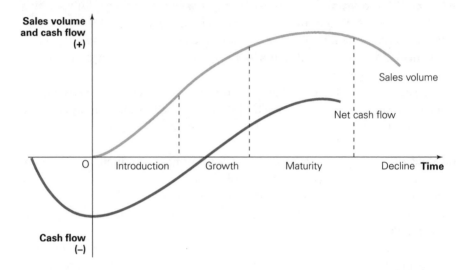

The product life cycle has a familiar pattern, but its duration varies considerably according to the nature of the product. Fashion clothing and a specific model of personal computer might have a life cycle of less than 3 years. Other products, such as Bovril, have a product life cycle of over 100 years and are still in the maturity stage.

■ *TIP* The product life cycle can be the basis of a strong line of analysis when linked to, for example, the marketing actions appropriate at each stage of the cycle and the financial implications for the business.

product orientation: where the managers of a business place great emphasis on the production process at the expense of marketing.

■ Product orientation is less common than it used to be, as an important part of being competitive is focusing on the needs of consumers. See *market orientation*.

■ *e.g.* Concorde is a classic example of a product supplied under a product-orientated philosophy. The technical achievement of manufacturing a supersonic airliner was more important than meeting consumers' needs.

product portfolio: mix or range of products supplied by a firm at a given time.

■ Firms aim to have products at various stages in the *product life cycle*, especially in fashion and technological industries where products quickly become obsolete. This requires businesses continuously to launch new products to help achieve steady sales over time. Firms can analyse their product portfolio using the *Boston matrix*, which categorises a business's products according to their market share and the growth rate of the market. As with the product life cycle, firms aim to have products in each of the classifications of the matrix.

profit: extent to which revenues exceed expenditures incurred in selling the product.

- The *profit and loss account* records more than a single type of profit. *Gross profit* is the revenue received from sales less the cost of the goods or services sold. This measure of profit does not deduct expenses such as advertising costs, rent and rates, and salaries of administration staff. *Net profit*, however, is sales revenue less all expenses. A third measure, *operating profit*, refers to profits generated from regular business activities and not one-off occurrences such as selling a property.

profit and loss account: financial statement recording a business's revenues and expenditures, and hence its profit or loss, over a stated period of time.

- Companies in the UK are legally obliged to produce a profit and loss account regularly. When read in conjunction with a business's *balance sheet*, a profit and loss account allows an analysis to be made of the financial performance of the enterprise. A profit and loss account is made up of three separate accounts, as illustrated below. See also *appropriation account*.

GOOCH & GOWER plc

Profit and loss account for the financial year ending 31 December (£000s)

Turnover (sales)		24,500	**Trading**
Cost of sales		(14,300)	**account**
GROSS PROFIT		10,200	
Distribution costs	435		
Administration expenses	646		
Selling expenses	348		**Profit**
Interest paid	150		**and loss**
		(1,579)	**account**
NET PROFIT ON ORDINARY ACTIVITIES BEFORE TAX		8,621	
Tax paid on ordinary activities		(1,983)	
NET PROFIT ON ORDINARY ACTIVITIES AFTER TAX		6,638	
Dividends paid and proposed		(2,244)	**Appropriation**
RETAINED PROFIT for the financial year		4,394	**account**

profit centre: part of an organisation's activities for which it is possible to calculate costs, revenues and hence profits.

- Profit centres might relate to a particular product, department or division, or even to the operations of a multinational in one particular country. Thus Ford (UK) could be regarded as a profit centre. By operating as a profit centre, managers and employees can have greater control over their financial affairs, and this increased authority might be a positive motivational factor. See also *cost centre*.

profit margin: selling price of a product less its cost of production.

- This is an important determinant of a business's profits and a factor that might be taken into account when setting the price of a product. The profit margin that a firm earns on a sale might depend upon the degree of competition in the market, consumers' perceptions of the product, and consumers' *price elasticity of demand*. See also *mark-up, gross profit margin* and *net profit margin*.

profit maximisation: an objective of many businesses to achieve the largest possible surplus of revenues over expenditures.

▦ Many firms in the *private sector* pursue profit maximisation as a primary *objective* and much economic theory concerning the behaviour of firms is based upon this assumption. Businesses trading with the single objective of profit maximisation operate in the interests of their *shareholders* (or other owners) rather than on behalf of the organisation's *stakeholders*.

profit quality: measure of the extent to which a particular type of profit is sustainable.

▦ Profits arising from non-trading activities (e.g. selling a fixed asset) might be regarded as of low quality because they are one-off. On the other hand, profits earned through developing a new product might be expected to continue and be adjudged high quality.

▦ *TIP* This can provide a useful argument for evaluation in many circumstances. It is not enough to consider the amount of profit made by a business; its quality should be judged too.

profit sharing: distributing some portion of a business's profits to its employees in addition to their regular wages or salaries.

▦ Profits might be distributed in the form of *cash* or *shares* in the business. The intention is to improve employee loyalty to the firm, thereby reducing *labour turnover* and improving employee morale and *motivation*. Profit sharing is a form of *performance-related pay*, but not one that discriminates effectively between the contributions made by individual employees.

promotion: how a business attempts to communicate with its customers and other interested parties, such as the media, trade unions and shareholders.

▦ Promotion consists of a number of elements: *advertising*, both persuasive and informative; *sales promotions* (e.g. giving free samples); *merchandising* (e.g. point-of-sale activities, such as display stands); direct marketing (i.e. communicating directly and interactively with consumers, and cutting out retailers); *public relations* (attempting to influence the public's perception of an organisation and its products through activities such as sponsorship, attending trade fairs and issuing press releases); and personal selling (where firms use sales teams to encourage customers to purchase their products). Firms use the parts of promotions that are appropriate to their circumstances and markets; this is known as the promotional mix.

▦ *e.g.* Direct Line has direct marketing at the heart of its promotional mix. Personal selling is common in the travel industry, where representatives of holiday firms visit travel agents regularly.

▦ *TIP* Do not fall into the old trap of believing that promotion is simply advertising. As you can see, there is a lot more to it than that.

prospectus: document issued by a company when offering *shares* or *debentures* for sale or when converting to *public limited company* status.

▥ The *Companies Acts* require a company to issue a prospectus in such circumstances. A prospectus provides information about the company, its financial history and the amount of capital to be raised. The business uses this publication to present itself as favourably as possible, without making any misleading statements (which are illegal). This is intended to allow potential investors to make an informed judgement.

protectionism: government policy favouring the use of measures designed to prevent the free entry of *imports* into a country.

▥ Protection can be achieved by placing taxes (or *tariffs*) on imports, increasing their price in relation to home-produced products. Alternatively, governments might use *quotas* that place a limit on the volume of a product that can be imported. Protection is intended to prevent domestic industries from facing the full force of international competition. It remains a controversial policy — many believe that it encourages inefficiency among firms subject to protection.

provisions: amount set aside and recorded in a business's accounts to protect it against some expected future expenditure.

▥ A business makes a provision rather than including a cost because it is not sure of the extent of the liability that it might incur.

▥ *e.g.* Businesses commonly make a provision in their accounts for *bad debts*, or for the tax they anticipate paying. Equally, a firm about to commence the process of *delayering* would be likely to make a provision for the costs of redundancy and retraining that might accompany restructuring.

PRP: see *performance-related pay*.

PSBR: see *public sector borrowing requirement*.

psychological pricing: tactic used in pricing intended to persuade consumers that prices are lower than they really are.

▥ At its simplest, this form of pricing entails charging £9.99 rather than £10 because the latter might represent a psychological barrier for consumers. This form of psychological pricing has been heavily used, but arguably it is falling out of favour as businesses such as Marks & Spencer price in round figures such as £20. A less well-known form of psychological pricing is prestige pricing, where a product is given a high price to persuade consumers of its quality.

public limited company (plc): large company that benefits from the opportunity to sell its *shares* on the *Stock Exchange* (or similar organised market).

▥ A public limited company is identified by the letters 'plc' after its name, reassuring investors that their liability is limited to the value of their investment. Public limited companies are required by the *Companies Acts* to provide considerable details of their financial performance for scrutiny by interested parties. This type of company is able to raise large amounts of capital because it can sell its shares freely. As a result, public limited companies are able to undertake research and development activities, purchase major fixed assets and produce on a large scale. See also *private limited company*.

public relations (PR): series of marketing activities intended to create favourable relationships between consumers and other groups that have an interest in an organisation.

■ PR activities include developing a positive *corporate image*, enhancing the organisation's social standing through *sponsorship* of sporting and arts events, and the management of relationships with the media. PR is a form of *communication* designed to persuade others of the standing and integrity of the business in question, with the aim of encouraging consumers to purchase its products and investors to buy (or hold on to) its shares. See also *promotion*.

public sector borrowing requirement (PSBR): extent to which the spending of central and local government and other public bodies exceeds their income.

■ This is an important indicator of a government's *fiscal policy*. A high (or increasing) PSBR normally indicates an expansionary fiscal policy, which is intended to increase the level of economic activity in the economy. The objective might be to reduce unemployment. Recent governments have operated with smaller PSBRs than in the past (reflecting a neutral fiscal policy) and have relied upon *monetary policy* to control the economy. At times, the government's income has exceeded its expenditure — a situation termed 'public sector debt repayment' (PSDR).

public spending: amount of expenditure by central and local governments and other public bodies.

■ This is an important element in a government's *fiscal policy*. Public expenditure can aid businesses by improving the infrastructure, making trading easier and more profitable, as well as by creating a demand for the products sold by businesses. The policy of *privatisation* has helped governments to control public expenditure in recent years.

PV: see *present value*.

qualitative research: form of *market research* intended to discover the attitudes and opinions of consumers that influence their purchasing behaviour.

■ Qualitative research is often based on very small samples and is gathered through discussion groups and interviews. By discovering why consumers behave in the ways they do, businesses can refine marketing decisions and the design of goods and services to make them more effective and appealing. See also *quantitative research*.

quality assurance: systems operated by organisations to ensure that all their products meet certain quality standards.

■ Quality assurance is about prevention: making sure that employees at each stage of production meet quality standards so that the final product satisfies consumers' needs. This philosophy emphasises the importance of employees producing goods and services conforming to standards on the first occasion. Under some quality assurance systems, importance is given to employees checking their own work to avoid sub-standard products slipping through. Firms can achieve British Standards award BS5750 (or its international equivalent ISO9000) for operating specified quality assurance systems.

■ *TIP* It is important to distinguish between quality assurance and *quality control*, and to use the terms precisely. The former is about prevention, while the latter is based on corrective action.

quality circle: where groups of workers meet regularly to identify methods of improving all aspects of the quality of their products.

■ Quality circles developed in Japan and consider working methods and the products themselves. They comprise 3–10 employees from all levels within the organisation, who assemble to discuss company problems and to propose solutions. Quality circles meet for 1–2 hours, two or three times a month, usually in working time. They are recognised as having a positive motivational impact upon employees as well as providing businesses with imaginative solutions to production problems.

quality control: system for checking completed products to ensure that they meet agreed standards.

■ Quality control takes place after the production process is complete to establish

123

q

whether products are of sufficient quality to meet the needs of consumers. The fact that quality control assumes that defects are inevitable has led firms to adopt *quality assurance* systems.

quango: stands for 'quasi-autonomous non-governmental organisation', an organisation or agency that is financed by a government but acts independently of it.

■ A quango is a national or regional public body that operates independently of ministers, but for which ministers are ultimately responsible.

■ *e.g.* the Low Pay Commission, which oversees the operation of the *minimum wage* and the Regional Development Agencies (RDAs). The RDAs are charged with producing regional economic strategies and undertaking various programmes aimed at regeneration, improving labour skills and improving the competitiveness of UK businesses.

quantitative research: collection of information that can be analysed statistically and expressed in numerical forms.

■ Quantitative research is intended to reveal information about sales figures, market size, prices that buyers are willing to pay and the characteristics of typical consumers. This form of *market research* can be collected through *primary research* (e.g. *questionnaires*) as well as from secondary sources (e.g. market reports). See also *qualitative research*.

questionnaire: set of questions in written form designed to collect information from large numbers of people.

■ This is a popular form of *primary research* and is frequently sent through the post for completion and return to the research team. A carefully constructed questionnaire can provide marketing teams with valuable information. Alternatively, questionnaires can be handed out at the *point-of-sale* or included as part of a product's *packaging*. While questionnaires can be a cheap form of research, businesses do not have much control over responses. Response rates for questionnaires can fall to below 10%. Firms often offer incentives, such as entry to a prize draw, to overcome this.

quota: restriction, imposed by governments, on the quantity of a particular product that can be imported.

■ Governments can control the amount of a product being imported by issuing a limited number of licences to import. Quotas are used by governments pursuing a policy of *protectionism*, usually with the aim of encouraging the development of a particular industry. See also *tariffs*.

quota sample: type of *sampling* in which a proportion of the total sample should comprise respondents possessing certain characteristics.

■ It is usual for the make-up of a quota sample to reflect the structure of the market at which the firm is aiming its products. Researchers conducting quota samples are given clear instructions on the number of respondents to survey in each quota sample.

■ *e.g.* A *market research* team might decide that a particular sample they wish to survey should contain 4,000 women aged 20–50 and working, 5,000 women in full-time employment of any adult age, and 2,000 women not in full-time employment.

quotation: statement (usually in written form) setting out the price and other terms on which a business is prepared to supply specific products.

■ It is common for businesses to ask for quotations from a number of suppliers in order to find the lowest price, subject to certain standards, such as meeting delivery dates. The greater the proposed expenditure, the more likely it is that a firm will seek quotations before spending its money.

R&D: see *research and development*.

random sample: selection of a group of consumers (or firms or products) from a larger population, giving each person (or firm or product) an equal chance of being included in the sample.

■ This type of *sampling* should provide a sample that is representative of the larger population. Thus the analysis of the results of a random sample should give results that would have been achieved if the entire population had been surveyed.

■ *e.g.* A retailer might survey customers about the level of service given by staff in its outlets by choosing to interview every twentieth customer passing through its stores at varied times of the week.

ratio analysis: technique for analysing a business's financial performance by comparing one piece of accounting information with another.

■ Ratios can be used to analyse a business's profitability, *liquidity* and efficiency over a period of time or in comparison with other firms or industry standard figures. Ratio analysis is conducted using data primarily available on a firm's *balance sheet* and *profit and loss account*. While the technique does allow a quantitative assessment of a firm's performance, it ignores many other factors, such as the quality of the business's workforce, its market position and the state of the economy.

■ *TIP* Students often get so involved in calculating ratios that they fail to appreciate the meaning of the results. You should know for each ratio what constitutes a good result and what figure might be unacceptable.

rationalisation: reducing the productive capacity of a business.

■ Firms reduce their productive capacity by closing factories or offices, selling surplus fixed assets and making redundant those employees who are no longer required. Firms will only undertake rationalisation if they believe that their *excess capacity* is a long-term problem. Rationalisation is not an appropriate solution when a business is faced with short-term fluctuations in the level of demand for its products.

■ *TIP* The term 'rationalisation' is sometimes used to describe circumstances in which firms reorganise to increase their efficiency. However, *restructuring* is a more accurate term for such a situation.

raw data: collected data that have not been organised numerically.

■ A business might collect a great deal of data as part of a *market research* programme. Until the data have been organised (perhaps by arranging them into classes and presenting them graphically), they remain raw data. It is not possible to interpret data in their raw form or to take marketing decisions based upon them.

real income: earnings of individuals or organisations adjusted for the effects of price changes.

■ Real income measures an individual or organisation's ability to purchase goods and services (their 'purchasing power'). Real income or wages are important concepts in wage negotiations, as employees are interested in the rise in their real wages and not in their money wages (unadjusted for *inflation*).

■ *e.g.* If a manager's salary rises by 5% in one year, but at the same time inflation is 3%, the rise in real income enjoyed by the manager is approximately 2%.

receiver: person responsible for taking control of an insolvent business and making the necessary arrangements to pay *creditors*.

■ The receiver is notified by a court of a *bankruptcy* or winding-up order against an enterprise. He or she will then be responsible for administering the *insolvency* case. This might involve trying to sell the business as a going concern, if possible. Alternatively, the receiver might decide to close it down and sell off the remaining *assets* to pay as much of the business's debts as possible. A business administered by a receiver is said to be 'in receivership'.

recession: period of time during which the level of activity in the economy is declining.

■ This means that *production* levels might be falling, *unemployment* rising and consumer spending declining. These symptoms might worsen if the recession deepens. Recessions occur irregularly, but at approximately 7–9-year intervals. A recession occurs during the downswing stage of the *business cycle*. Businesses supplying luxury products might experience significant falls in demand during a recession, while those selling necessities might be little affected. Governments use *fiscal policy* and *monetary policy* to attempt to alleviate the worst effects of recessions.

recruitment: finding and appointing new employees.

■ Firms might carry out the recruitment process themselves or use the professional services of recruitment agencies. Recruitment might be internal, by promoting or redeploying existing employees, or external, by recruiting any suitably qualified candidates. The number and type of employees to be recruited will be established by the labour needs set out in the organisation's human resource plan.

■ *TIP* Recruitment can be an expensive process for businesses. However, it is often a good line of argument to present this (and the costs of training) as an investment. Investment in human resources can pay rich dividends.

redeployment: reassigning employees to new duties within the organisation.

■ Sometimes this might require employees to move to a new location; on other occasions, employees remain in the same office or factory following redeployment. Redeployment allows businesses to avoid demotivating their workforce through using *redundancy*. It also avoids the costs of making employees redundant. However, redeployment is likely to require considerable expenditure on *training* to assist employees in carrying out new duties efficiently.

reducing balance method: method of writing down the value of *assets* over time by removing a fixed percentage of their value each year.

■ This method of *depreciation* removes a larger proportion of an asset's value in the early years of its life. Reducing balance is an appropriate method of depreciation for assets that lose a higher proportion of their value in their early years and which are not retained for the whole of their useful working life (e.g. vehicles). See also *straight-line depreciation*.

■ *e.g.* The table below shows the effect of the reducing balance method for an articulated lorry that initially cost £100,000 and is depreciated by 20% each year.

Year	Depreciation allowance (£)	Asset's book value (at year's end) (£)
1	20,000	80,000
2	16,000	64,000
3	12,800	51,200
4	10,240	40,960

redundancy: where employment is terminated because the type of labour offered by the employee(s) in question is surplus to requirements.

■ Workers might be made redundant because their skills have become obsolete, because demand for the business's product has declined, or because the business is closing down. Employees who are made redundant are entitled to compensation in the form of redundancy pay according to age and length of service.

■ *TIP* Although we talk about making employees redundant, technically speaking the employee is not made redundant; it is the job that no longer exists as a result of redundancy.

regional policy: series of government initiatives intended to promote prosperity in less wealthy regions of the UK.

■ Regional policy is based upon the identification of certain less prosperous areas in the UK that suffer lower incomes and higher unemployment than most other parts of the country. Firms relocating and creating employment in development areas receive Regional Selective Assistance (RSA) grants. Smaller firms (with fewer than 25 employees) might receive Regional Enterprise Grants for creating or maintaining jobs. The *European Union* also operates a regional policy with the objective of supporting poorer regions across Europe. See also *location* and *assisted areas*.

■ *e.g.* Great Yarmouth and Lowestoft on the east coast of England comprise a designated region, known as a development area.

registered capital: see *authorised share capital*.

Registrar of Companies: public official responsible for maintaining detailed records of all limited companies registered in the UK.

■ The Registrar of Companies oversees the operation of Companies House and fulfils three main functions: the *incorporation*, re-registration and striking-off of companies; the registration of documents that must be filed under company, insolvency and related legislation (e.g. *Articles of Association* and *Memorandum of Association*); and the provision of company information to the public.

regulation: control of some aspect of business activity, normally by the government or another official body.

■ Regulations are rules that impinge on many aspects of business operations. They are usually part of a piece of legislation, but might also take the form of a *voluntary code of practice*. In general, recent governments have tried to reduce the number of regulations that firms face in the hope of promoting greater enterprise and efficiency. See also *deregulation*.

■ *e.g.* The selling of financial services (mortgages, insurance policies, etc.) is subject to strict regulation governed by the Financial Services Act and monitored by the Financial Services Authority (FSA). The government established OFGAS and OFWAT to regulate the activities of the privatised gas and water utilities (especially checking that prices are not set too high).

reorder level: quantity of *stock* at which an order is generated for replacement items.

■ The quantity decided upon for a reorder level will depend upon the rate at which the stock is used up, the time taken to supply new stock (the *lead time*) and the cost of holding stock. Increasingly, businesses are seeking to minimise their holdings of stocks (through systems such as *just-in-time*) to minimise costs. See *stock control*.

research and development (R&D): the scientific investigation necessary to discover new products and the process of bringing these products on to the market.

■ Research might take the form of brainstorming ideas or work in a laboratory. Firms in industries such as pharmaceuticals and computer software spend enormous sums on research and development. The intention is to gain a competitive advantage by offering products that are better designed and more technologically advanced, and that meet consumer needs more than those of competitors.

■ *TIP* Do not confuse research and development with *market research*. R&D is based on scientific investigation, while market research discovers the needs and opinions of consumers.

reserves: the part of the profits earned by a company each year that it decides to retain.

■ This money is used to purchase additional *fixed assets*, thereby increasing the value of the company as well as its potential to generate income. As a result of this reinvestment of profits, the worth of shareholders' investment in the company will normally increase in the long term.

■ *TIP* The concept of reserves is frequently misunderstood. Although reserves are made up of *retained profit*, they are not held in the form of cash. They are invested in the business, rather than being held as savings.

residual value: worth of a *fixed asset* at the end of its working life.

■ It might be that the asset has no value, has some scrap value or can be sold to another enterprise as the business seeks more productive assets. Thus a business might purchase a delivery vehicle and sell it when it becomes unreliable but still has some value. Alternatively, the firm might retain the vehicle and sell it for scrap when it becomes unroadworthy. Residual value is an important element in calculating *depreciation*. See also *straight-line depreciation*.

restrictive practice: any business policy that reduces the level of competition within a market, consequently disadvantaging consumers.

■ Restrictive practices have to be registered with the Restrictive Practices Court if they are to be legal. Eight criteria (known as 'gateways') exist under which restrictive practices may be judged legal if they are in the consumer's interest. Restrictive practices are deemed illegal unless their legality can be proved.

■ *e.g.* *collusion* between firms to share markets or to fix prices at some level; dominant firms forcing retailers to sell their products at some minimum price, preventing consumers enjoying the benefits of special offers; large businesses refusing to supply retailers unless they stock the full range of the firm's products.

■ *TIP* Another form of restrictive practice exists that can cause confusion. Restrictive labour practices limit the free use of labour within an organisation. For example, demarcation might mean that rigid controls are placed on the duties that particular employees can carry out.

restructuring: changing the way in which an enterprise is organised.

■ Restructuring might mean that some jobs are eliminated, that others are created and that the business's *organisational structure* is redrawn. New lines of authority and communication are created. Businesses commonly restructure in response to some external change, and to improve their efficiency.

■ *e.g.* In recent years, many organisations have *delayered*, reducing the number of *levels of hierarchy* in the business. The aim is to reduce labour costs and improve motivation and productivity by offering junior employees greater control over their working lives.

retail audit: technique of *market research* whereby a firm's employees visit selected shops to investigate the sales patterns of its products.

■ Retail audits provide firms with important information: sales of particular brands by different types of retail outlet (e.g. corner shops, hypermarkets); stocks of the firm's products held (in comparison with those of rival businesses); and selling prices in different outlets, including discounts available. They help businesses to identify market trends as early as possible and to take appropriate action.

retail price index (RPI) (also called 'headline rate of inflation'): official measure of the rate of *inflation* based upon the changes in prices of a bundle of goods and services.

▓ This index measures the average change each month in the prices of about 600 products purchased by households in the UK. Each month 12,000 calculations are completed to construct the index.

retained profit (also called 'ploughed-back profit'): that part of a firm's profit after tax that is not distributed, but reinvested in the business.

▓ A business's decisions regarding the distribution of profit are recorded on the *appropriation account* within the *profit and loss account*. A decision to retain a high proportion of profits after tax is likely to result in shareholders receiving lower dividends, but should encourage the long-term growth of the business. Retained profit is a vital source of finance for businesses intending to invest in *fixed assets*.

return on capital employed (ROCE) (also called 'primary efficiency ratio'): important measure of the efficiency of a business obtained by comparing *operating profits* with the *capital employed* by the organisation.

▓ ROCE is calculated using the following formula:

$$\text{return on capital employed} = \frac{\text{operating profit}}{\text{capital employed}} \times 100\%$$

It represents an important measure of a firm's profitability. Higher figures for ROCE are preferable. The return on capital should exceed the rate of interest available on interest-bearing accounts with banks and building societies, which represent a risk-free investment. The ROCE for a business should be compared with those achieved in previous years and by other firms in the same industry.

▓ *TIP* The term 'capital employed' needs careful definition if ROCE is to be calculated accurately. It includes ordinary and preference *share capital, reserves, debentures* and long-term loans.

revenue: income received by a firm from the sale of its goods and services.

▓ Revenue received is an important determinant of the profits earned by a business. Some firms have revenue maximisation as an *objective*.

revenue budget (also called 'sales revenue budget'): financial forecast of the income expected by a business, or part of a business, over some specified period of time.

▓ A revenue budget is based upon a business's forecast sales multiplied by the expected selling price. It is normally expressed in terms of anticipated monthly revenue. A revenue budget is constructed using the results of *market research* as well as the experience of previous years. See also *budgets*.

▓ *TIP* Constructing the revenue budget is an important part of the process of budgeting. Once the expected sales have been established, a business is able to plan its production and draw up its expenditure budgets.

revenue expenditure: purchase of day-to-day items (e.g. wages, fuel, raw materials and stock) that will be used up in a short time.

■ Such expenditure is recorded on a firm's *profit and loss account*. See also *capital expenditure*.

rights issue: issue of new *shares* offered to *shareholders* in proportion to their existing holdings at a discounted price.

■ It is common for businesses to offer shareholders the chance to purchase one new share for every eight already held, at a discount of, say, 15% on the current market price. Rights issues are a relatively cheap method of raising additional capital and are considerably less expensive than selling shares to the general public by issuing a *prospectus*. A company's share price often declines after a rights issue.

risk capital: see *venture capital*.

ROCE: see *return on capital employed*.

royalty: payment made in return for some privilege or right.

■ Royalties are granted to authors for the right to publish and sell their work or to the holders of a *patent* for the right to use their idea. Royalties are also paid for the rights to some physical assets, such as mineral resources. The term 'royalties' arose because the Crown first granted them.

RPI: see *retail price index*.

salary: money paid to an employee for his or her labour services, usually expressed as an annual figure.

■ Salaries are not normally linked to a specific number of hours each week, but are paid to employees carrying out professional or management roles in an organisation. They are usually paid each month, in contrast to *wages*, which are paid weekly. Salaries can be gross (before the deduction of taxes and national insurance) or net (after deductions have taken place). Salaries often constitute a fixed cost element of a business's labour expenses, in that they do not vary with the firm's level of output.

sale and leaseback: sale by a business of a *fixed asset*, before renting it back from the new owner.

■ A number of businesses, especially retailers, sell their properties before leasing them back. Sale and leaseback offers a business an injection of capital while the business retains the use of the asset.

■ *e.g.* In 2000, the House of Fraser completed a deal selling 15 stores for an estimated £170 million.

■ *TIP* Sale and leaseback is an important method of improving *cash flow*, but one that should be used cautiously in examination answers. It is often the case that the expenditure incurred in leasing the asset over a long period exceeds the capital inflow from the asset's sale.

sales promotion: range of short-term *marketing* tactics designed to encourage purchases by consumers.

■ Sales promotions can be used to increase the *market share* held by a product, to renew interest in a product or to defend a product's market position against the actions of a competitor. The success of sales promotions depends heavily on firms persuading retailers to stock their products.

■ *e.g.* in-store displays, 'two for the price of one' offers, demonstrations and competitions.

■ *TIP* Sales promotion has a different meaning from *promotion*. The latter covers a wider range of marketing activities, including advertising, public relations and personal selling as well as sales promotions.

sales revenue: income received by a firm from the sale of its goods and services.

A business's sales revenue is the first item recorded on its *profit and loss account*. It is an important determinant of the profits earned by a business. Some firms have revenue maximisation as an *objective*. See also *sales volume*.

sales revenue budget: see *revenue budget*.

sales volume: quantity or volume of products sold by a firm over a period of time.

Sales volume is one of two factors determining the revenue received by a business:

> revenue = sales volume × selling price

Sales volumes have important implications for those responsible for managing and scheduling production. An increase in sales volume might pose problems for businesses with little or no *excess capacity*. The term 'sales volume' is sometimes used in relation to the quantity of products sold by an entire industry.

sampling: selection of a representative group of consumers (or firms or products) from a larger population.

Sampling is commonly used as a source of data on consumer needs and behaviour because businesses cannot afford to research every potential customer within their market. The evidence gathered from analysing the sample is used to predict what might happen in relation to the entire population: for example, how consumers might respond to a new product. A number of different methods of sampling exist, including *random samples* and *quota samples*. A dilemma facing marketing departments is that large samples might provide more accurate information but will be more expensive.

TIP The results of all samples will contain errors because they will not entirely reflect the larger population. Those taking marketing decisions have to take this into account.

satisficing: business objective whereby a firm aims to make a level of profits that is less than the maximum attainable.

Businesses might settle for profits less than the highest possible for a number of reasons. The owner of a small business might consider reasonable amounts of leisure time more important than earning further profits. On the other hand, a large firm might deliberately reduce its price, forgoing short-term profit, in pursuit of increasing market share.

scale: level of production achieved by a firm.

Scale is an important issue for many businesses because of the existence of *economies of scale* and *diseconomies of scale*. Firms can achieve considerable competitive advantage from producing at a scale or output that minimises costs. Scale is particularly important in industries such as steel making and retailing, where firms incur heavy *fixed costs*. In such industries, large volumes of output are essential to reduce *unit costs* and the price at which the product can be sold.

e.g. The following table shows how a business with heavy fixed costs reaps enormous benefits in terms of falling costs per unit as it increases its scale. This offers managers greater flexibility in pricing decisions.

Level of output	Fixed costs (£000s)	Variable costs (£000s)	Total costs (£000s)	Cost per unit of output (£000s)
100	5,000	100	5,100	51.00
500	5,000	450	5,450	10.90
1,000	5,000	910	5,910	5.91
2,000	5,000	1,805	6,805	3.40
5,000	5,000	4,480	9,480	1.90
10,000	5,000	8,870	13,870	1.39

scientific school of management: approach to management that places great emphasis on the use of quantifiable data and the careful design of jobs.

■ Supporters of this school of thought believe that jobs should be designed as a result of studying employees in the workplace. Using the most efficient workers as models, jobs should be designed to contain a limited number of straight-forward tasks carried out repeatedly and under close supervision. The school believes that employees are motivated solely by money and that the pay system should be designed to encourage greater productivity. One of the best-known members of this school is Frederick *Taylor*. These views are in sharp contrast to those held by the *human relations* school of management.

■ **TIP** It is easy to criticise this approach to management. However, it might be appropriate in certain circumstances — for example, when dealing with large numbers of unskilled employees who are carrying out simple tasks. It should not be dismissed out of hand.

seasonal unemployment: *unemployment* that exhibits regular and predictable fluctuations throughout the year.

■ This type of unemployment results from the seasonal pattern of demand or supply experienced by certain industries (e.g. agriculture, tourism and construction). All of these industries require more labour during the summer months and lay off employees during the winter. Some regions, notably rural areas and areas popular with tourists, suffer heavily from this form of unemployment. Seasonal unemployment can be difficult to counteract. See also *cyclical unemployment, frictional unemployment* and *structural unemployment*.

seasonal variation: regular and repeated patterns in data that appear at the same time in successive years.

■ Although seasonal variation is normally discussed on an annual basis, it can also be observed over shorter periods of time. Many retailers report their highest sales on Friday and Saturday. The fluctuations in data associated with seasonal variation can make it difficult to analyse trends in data such as sales and

S

production figures. By using statistical techniques such as *moving averages*, seasonal variation can be eliminated.

■ *e.g.* The output of many industries declines during July and August when most employees take their annual holidays.

secondary data: information that already exists in some form, having been collected for a different purpose and possibly by a different organisation.

■ Secondary data are cheaper to collect than *primary data*, but might be less up-to-date and less appropriate for the firm's purposes.

■ *e.g.* government statistics on production and consumer expenditure, internal company data on sales and stocks, and information published by market research agencies, such as Mintel.

secondary research: form of *market research* in which businesses use *secondary data*.

■ *TIP* It is possible to analyse the value of a particular form of market research by using criteria such as the importance of having accurate data or gathering data quickly. Do not assume that secondary research and data will always be 'second best'. They might be most suitable for a firm requiring quick results.

secondary sector: those firms in the economy that convert raw materials into finished goods.

■ The secondary sector of the economy is really another way of describing manufacturing industry. The twentieth century saw a decline in the relative importance of the secondary sector in the UK economy. In common with most other advanced economies, the production of services has become more important in the UK and there has been a corresponding decline in manufacturing. By 2000, manufacturing output accounted for less than 20% of the *gross national product* of the UK. See *primary sector* and *tertiary sector*.

self-employed: a person who is in business on his or her own account rather than being employed by a separate organisation.

■ Self-employment offers individuals greater control over their working lives and the full benefits of their labours. However, it is less secure than being employed by an organisation. Over 3% of the UK's workforce was self-employed in 2000.

■ *e.g.* Self-employment is common in professions such as accountancy, in the construction industry and among authors.

semi-variable costs: those expenses incurred by a business that have fixed and variable elements.

■ *e.g.* the expenses associated with a business's delivery vehicle. Costs such as insurance and road tax are *fixed costs*, as they are unlikely to alter irrespective of the amount the vehicle is used. However, fuel and servicing represent *variable costs*, as they vary proportionately with the vehicle's usage.

■ *TIP* The existence of semi-variable costs can pose problems when conducting a *break-even* analysis. This can be offered as a shortcoming of the technique of break even.

share: document representing the ownership of part of a company.

▓ Purchasers of shares receive a share certificate in return for their payment to the company. Shares are an *investment* carrying risk but offering returns in the form of *dividends* or an increase in the *market price* of the shares. The risk exists because shares might fall in value. The shares of *public limited companies* can be purchased and sold on the *Stock Exchange*. Shares in *private limited companies* are traded privately with the agreement of all the *shareholders* of the business. Two main types of share exist: *ordinary shares* and *preference shares*.

share capital: money invested into a limited company as a consequence of the sale of *shares*.

▓ A business's share capital represents a permanent source of funds because if individual *shareholders* wish to recoup their investment, they sell the shares to another individual or organisation. Thus ownership is transferred while the capital remains with the company. Share capital is an important *source of finance* for companies, particularly because it does not receive a fixed payment; *dividends* can be reduced in years when profits are low.

▓ *TIP* Although the sale of shares is an attractive option in many ways, some small private companies might be reluctant to take this step because the existing owners might lose control of the business if a large number of additional shares are sold.

shareholder: person or organisation that owns *shares* in a company.

▓ Although shareholders own a company, their control is limited because only a minority attend *annual general meetings* and have detailed business knowledge. Only the holders of *ordinary shares* have the right to vote at company meetings. Some of the largest shareholders in the UK are insurance companies (e.g. Prudential). Such institutional investors use the money subscribed by policy holders to purchase enormous numbers of shares in diverse companies, in the expectation of making a profit as shares rise in value. See also *divorce of ownership from control*.

shareholders' funds: that part of a company's long-term finance that belongs to its *shareholders*.

▓ Shareholders' funds are made up of the *capital* invested in the business plus any *reserves* that have been accumulated through retaining profits over the years. Shareholders' funds are recorded on a company's *balance sheet*.

share options: opportunity for employees (usually senior employees) to purchase *shares* in the company at a fixed price.

▓ Share options offer certain employees the chance to buy company shares at some point in the future, but at the current market price. Employees cannot lose from share options because if the share price is below the option price at the appointed date, they will not take up the option. Share options are generally regarded as a management perk. A survey in 1999 revealed that about 14% of UK companies operated share option schemes.

■ *e.g.* Assume a company's current share price is £2. A manager might be given the option to purchase 5,000 shares in 2 years' time at this price. Two years later, if the company's share price has risen to £3, the manager could exercise her option and sell the shares for an immediate profit of £5,000: (£3 − £2) × 5,000 shares. If the share price is below £2, she will not take up the option.

share premium: surplus received by companies when they issue new *shares* at a price in excess of their face value.

■ *e.g.* A company might have issued 8 million of its 10 million shares at their face or par value of £1 each. After 3 years' successful trading, the business might decide to issue the remaining 2 million shares to fund a particular capital project. However, in the intervening period the market price of the company's shares might have risen to £1.50. In these circumstances, the share premium on a single share will be 50p — market price less the share's face value. The company will raise £3 million as a result of the share issue, of which £1 million will represent the total share premium.

shop-floor: lowest level in an *organisational structure*.

■ This term has a manufacturing origin. The shop-floor was that part of a factory that held the machinery and the workers directly engaged in production — the most junior employees. Nowadays it refers more generally to the lowest rung in an organisation, irrespective of the nature of the business.

shop steward: representative of a *trade union* in an organisation, who has been elected by the members of that union.

■ Shop stewards can form an important *communication channel* between management and employees, and participate in *collective bargaining* over pay and working conditions. They might also represent individual employees in grievance and disciplinary proceedings and hold responsibilities regarding health and safety in the workplace. Shop stewards also recruit new members to the union and communicate with regional officials.

significance testing: verifying the accuracy of the results in a *sampling* exercise.

■ It is normal to seek 95% certainty that the results of the sample reflect accurately the population as a whole.

simultaneous engineering: approach to *research and development* that allows firms to introduce new products onto the market more quickly.

■ Simultaneous engineering is an aspect of *Japanisation* that organises R&D so that various stages of the process are completed at the same time rather than consecutively. For example, certain testing stages might be conducted while further design is taking place. By reducing the time required to introduce the product, development costs are lessened and the firm receives a competitive advantage from being on the market earlier.

single European currency: common currency (the euro) that is intended for use throughout the nations of the *European Union*.

■ On 1 January 1999, the euro was introduced into 11 EU states: Austria,

Belgium, Finland, France, Germany, Ireland, Italy, Luxembourg, the Netherlands, Portugal and Spain. These states will continue to use their domestic notes and coins until euro notes and coins are available on 1 January 2002. The countries introducing the euro have tied the exchange values of their currencies together and co-ordinated economic policies in preparation for the new currency. The UK has delayed a decision on whether to join the single European currency. There are a number of advantages to businesses if the UK adopts the euro, not least that they would no longer have to pay commission to convert pounds into other European currencies.

■ **TIP** Although *exchange rates* (and hence prices) are an important determinant of competitiveness, many non-price factors, such as quality and design, also play a significant part. This can be an important line of analysis when considering the factors affecting the *international competitiveness* of a business.

single sourcing: purchase of raw materials and components from just one supplier.

■ Single sourcing makes the supplier an integral part of the production process. This is a common policy for firms adopting a *just-in-time* production strategy and its success relies upon the development of excellent communications (and a high degree of trust) between the supplier and the producer. Producers can benefit from discounts for bulk orders and high-quality service from suppliers. However, this type of arrangement involves a degree of risk because if, for any reason, the supplier cannot fulfil any orders, the producer has no alternative source of components and materials.

single status: ending discrimination between different grades of employees in an organisation by providing the same facilities and benefits for all.

■ Under single status, all employees use the same restaurant, resting areas and car parks, work the same hours and benefit from the same sick pay and holiday arrangements. By blurring the distinction between all grades of employees, businesses expect lower *labour turnover* and improved *motivation* among *shop-floor* employees. Single status is an aspect of *Japanisation*.

single union agreement: arrangement under which a business only recognises one *trade union* for the purpose of negotiating wages and working conditions.

■ This type of agreement has become more common in the UK as the skill requirements of certain industries have changed, making some unions obsolete in the workplace. For example, print workers play a much less important role in the newspaper industry than was formerly the case. Single union deals offer benefits to employers in terms of more straightforward *collective bargaining*, ending the complexities of dealing with several unions simultaneously. However, such agreements have resulted in inter-union disputes and encouraged the growth of *general unions*.

sleeping partner: individual who contributes capital to a *partnership*, but does not play an active role in the management of the enterprise.

■ The Partnership Act of 1907 granted sleeping (or dormant) partners the opportunity to receive the privilege of *limited liability*. If they take up an active part in the running of the business, they forgo this privilege.

slump: stage of the *business cycle* during which the level of economic activity falls to its lowest point before recovering.

■ This period is characterised by high levels of *unemployment* and *bankruptcy*, low levels of production and consumer spending, and attempts by the government to stimulate economic recovery by, for example, reducing *interest rates*. A slump might follow on from a *recession* (or a downswing in the business cycle), but this is not always the case. Government actions, such as reducing interest rates and increasing its own spending, can prevent a recession developing into a slump.

■ *TIP* Not all businesses pass through the business cycle at the same time. Construction often enters into and recovers from a slump before other industries. Any analysis of the effects of a business cycle should take into account the nature of the business.

social audit: independent investigation into the effects of a firm's activities upon society in general.

■ Social audits consider the impact of the firm's operations on the *health and safety* of its workforce and on the environment, in terms of pollution, waste disposal and the recycling of materials. They are most common in those sectors of the economy where the potential to cause pollution and generate other social costs is the greatest.

■ *e.g.* Oil companies such as Shell and BP publish their social audits.

■ *TIP* Social audits are a form of *public relations* for some businesses, which use them to gain a competitive advantage rather than to minimise their negative effects on society.

Social Charter: series of measures intended to improve and harmonise employment legislation in the EU.

■ Although the Charter is described as a social measure, it primarily covers employment matters. Key elements include limiting the length of the working week, providing access to vocational *training* for employees, and offering employees the opportunity to participate in decision making. The UK signed up to the Social Charter in 1997 after delaying a decision on it. Some critics of the Charter have argued that it will damage the *international competitiveness* of UK firms by increasing their labour costs.

social class: classification of society based upon the occupations, interests, perceptions and beliefs of individuals.

■ Placing people into groups with common characteristics enables marketing managers to communicate effectively with target audiences. Firms produce goods for certain social groups: for example, broadsheet newspapers such as the *Independent* are primarily aimed at social classes A and B.

■ *TIP* The government has recently produced a new classification of social classes for use in the UK. This has more categories than the old Jicnar's scale.

Class	Description	Examples
Class 1	1.1 Employers in large organisations	1.1 Corporate managers
	1.2 Higher professionals	1.2 Doctors, lawyers
Class 2	Lower managerial and professional	Journalists, actors, nurses
Class 3	Intermediate occupations	Secretary, driving instructor
Class 4	Small employers and own account workers	Publicans, taxi drivers
Class 5	Lower supervisory and craft occupations	Plumbers, butchers, train drivers
Class 6	Semi-routine occupations	Shop assistants, traffic wardens
Class 7	Routine occupations	Waiter, road sweeper
Class 8	Never worked and long-term unemployed	

social cost: total cost of a good or service, including costs borne by society in general as well as those borne by the organisation engaged in production.

■ The formula for the social cost of a good is:

$$\text{social cost} = \begin{array}{c}\text{private costs}\\\text{(borne by the firm)}\end{array} + \begin{array}{c}\text{externalities}\\\text{(costs borne by}\\\text{others in society)}\end{array}$$

Not all goods incur social costs, but many do. Governments attempt to curb externalities by using legislation.

■ *e.g.* A chemical company might pay for the labour and raw materials used in production, but others pay the costs of pollution that result from the manufacturing process. For example, a nearby fish farm might lose stock because of chemicals in the water.

social responsibility: philosophy under which businesses consider the interests of all groups in society as a central part of their decision making.

■ Businesses operating this philosophy take into account the interests and needs of all their *stakeholders* rather than just focusing on maximising profits for their *shareholders*. Socially responsible actions reduce profits in the short term, but they can enhance a business's *corporate image*, assisting its long-term profitability.

■ *e.g.* A socially responsible firm might use more expensive but sustainable sources of raw materials or provide play facilities for local children.

sole trader: business owned by a single person.

■ Sole traders are common in industries such as hairdressing, painting and decorating, and retailing. Although only one person owns and is responsible for the business, other people might be employed. It is simple and cheap to set up as a sole trader, and there are few legal formalities. However, about 80% of sole traders fail within 5 years of commencing trading. Common reasons for failure are lack of capital and insufficient management knowledge and experience.

solvency: where a business is able to meet its financial obligations at the time they are due.

■ A solvent business has *assets* that exceed its *liabilities* and is able to pay its way both in the short term and in the long term. It is illegal for a business to continue trading if it is not solvent. See also *insolvency*.

sources of finance: ways in which a business raises funds for use in the short and long term.

■ Short-term sources of finance include *overdrafts* and *trade credit,* while organisations requiring funds for longer periods might sell *shares* or arrange a *mortgage*. Businesses need external finance to establish themselves, to operate on a day-to-day basis and to grow. Planning to meet the financial needs of a business is an important aspect of management.

■ *TIP* Questions asking about possible sources of finance are very common in business studies examinations. It is important to propose sources of finance that are appropriate to the type of business (e.g. partnerships cannot sell shares) and to the amount of funds required (venture capitalists will not provide large sums of money). Some situations require long-term finance, while in other cases short-term sources will suffice.

span of control: number of subordinates directly supervised by a manager.

■ The popularity of *delayering* has led to organisations operating with wider spans of control than in the past. The disadvantage of this is that supervision is bound to relax. The maximum number of employees a manager can supervise effectively is estimated to be six.

■ *e.g.* In the following diagram, manager A has a span of control of three because only employees B, C and D are responsible to him or her. The other employees report directly to other *line managers*. Manager F has the largest span of control, with five staff reporting to him or her.

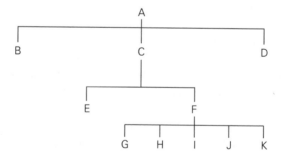

■ *TIP* Don't forget that the size of a typical span of control in an organisation is related to the number of *levels of hierarchy*. The more levels of hierarchy a business removes, the wider the resulting spans of control are likely to be. At some point, the advantages of giving greater authority to employees through *delayering* will be outweighed by a lack of supervision and co-ordination.

special order decision: where a business has to decide whether to accept orders at a price different from that usually charged.

▣ Two types of special order decision exist. First, there is the offer of a price in excess of the normal selling price. This might sound attractive, but customers willing to pay more than the going rate might have special requirements that create additional costs for the supplier. The effect of the order on profits should be assessed carefully before reaching a decision. Second, there are orders requesting a lower than normal price. These might be worth accepting if the selling price covers the *variable costs* and the business has sufficient capacity to fulfil the order without incurring extra *fixed costs*.

sponsorship: where a business gives financial or other support to individuals, teams, events or organisations that are not part of the sponsor's normal trading activities.

▣ Those engaging in sponsorship do so as part of their promotional mix in the hope of improving their *corporate image* (and sales) through association with sport, the arts or a charitable event.

▣ *e.g.* Sponsorship is commonplace in sport and the arts. Cadbury's sponsors the television programme **Coronation Street** and Virgin sponsors an annual concert of popular music. In 2000, Manchester United agreed a sponsorship deal with Vodafone worth over £30 million to the club over a 4-year period.

stakeholder: any individual or group having an interest or 'stake' in the activities and performance of an organisation.

▣ Stakeholders include employees, customers, suppliers, *shareholders* and managers. Less obviously, local residents and government organisations such as the Inland Revenue are also stakeholders. All of these groups have an interest in the business, whether it is continued employment, high dividends and a rising share price, or regular and prompt payment of tax that is owed. It has become common for businesses to attempt to meet the needs of as many of their stakeholders as possible in order to generate a positive image. Such businesses place importance on fulfilling their *social responsibilities*.

▣ *TIP* It is appealing to think of businesses meeting their responsibilities to all their stakeholders. However, this is not easy to achieve — indeed, it might be impossible. Conflict between the needs of various groups is inevitable: for example, employees benefit from improved working conditions only at the expense of lower dividends for shareholders.

standard deviation: measure of the degree of scatter (or variation) in a group of data.

▣ It is common, in some groups of data, for numbers to cluster around the *mean*; in other groups, the data are further away. The standard deviation measures the extent of the variation from the mean. In business, the standard deviation is important in interpreting the results of *market research* and in relation to *quality control*. The basic formula for the standard deviation (σ) is:

$$\sigma = \sqrt{\frac{\sum(x - \mu)^2}{n}}$$

where μ is the mean, x is the value of individual data in the series and n equals the number of pieces of data in the series. The symbol $\sum$ stands for 'the sum of', meaning that the mean has to be deducted from the value of each number in the data in a series of calculations.

standardisation: restricting the range of products supplied in an attempt to control costs.

■ Firms might only produce one product that they sell in all their markets. Coca-Cola only offers slight variation in the products it sells throughout the world, enabling it to produce in huge quantities in a limited number of locations. Standardisation offers firms the potential to benefit from *economies of scale* by concentrating production in a limited number of locations. The term can also refer to circumstances where all the products entering a particular market need to have standard features. For example, firms producing goods and services in the European Union have to meet common standards in relation to design, labelling and safety features.

sterling: name given to the UK's currency: the pound sterling.

■ This distinguishes it from the currencies of other nations that also use pounds. The word 'sterling' was originally used to identify coinage made from pure metals, and thus not debased in any way.

stock: (1) amount of raw materials, components, *work-in-progress* and finished goods held by a business at a given time.

■ Modern management techniques have sought to minimise holdings of stock as a means of reducing costs. See also *just-in-time*.

(2) fixed-interest security issued by the government as a means of raising long-term capital. The *Treasury*, acting on behalf of the government, sells stock in units of £100 on which a fixed rate of interest is paid each year, normally for a stated period of time.

■ Purchasers of government stock can recoup their investment by selling the security on the Stock Exchange or by waiting until the government repays the loan. Recently, the term has become more widely used to include *ordinary shares* issued by companies.

stock control: a number of systems used to regulate the quantity of *stock* held by a business.

■ The systems of stock control in existence vary, but all seek to minimise the costs of holding stocks while ensuring that the materials, components and finished goods are available when required. Modern methods of stock control have resulted in firms holding smaller quantities of stocks — or none at all. The key elements of a model of stock control are the *buffer stock* level, the *lead time*, the amount ordered and the *reorder level*. These are shown in the diagram below. See also *just-in-time*.

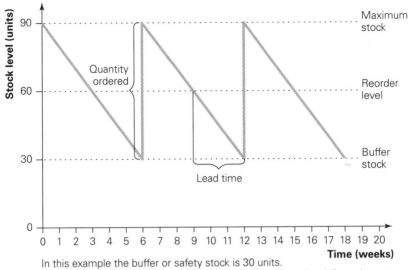

In this example the buffer or safety stock is 30 units.
The reorder level is 60 units, as supplies take 3 weeks to be delivered.

Stock Exchange: centre for trading financial securities such as *stocks* and *shares*.

■ The London Stock Exchange (LSE) is the main exchange in the UK, alongside a relatively new, smaller rival called Tradepoint, which offers shares in a limited but growing number of companies. Prior to the 1986 'big bang', the Stock Exchange operated a trading floor in Old Broad Street in the City of London. Trading was largely face-to-face between jobbers and stockbrokers. Post-1986, a technological revolution took hold. As a result, the bulk of trading was transferred to dealing screens. Large, open-plan trading rooms owned by banks and other international organisations became the order of the day. Electronic trading in stocks and shares (such as *Easdaq*) represents a growing form of competition to the Stock Exchange. See also *Alternative Investment Market*.

stock rotation: management of *stock* to avoid wastage due to deterioration and obsolescence.

■ By use of *first in, first out*, stock is automatically rotated and the oldest is used first.

■ *e.g.* Stock rotation is particularly important in industries where products are perishable, such as food retailing.

stock turnover: ratio that measures the number of times a business sells its average *stock* during a year.

■ Stock turnover is calculated using the formula:

$$\text{stock turnover} = \frac{\text{cost of goods sold}}{\text{average stock}}$$

The stock turnover figure for a business is expressed as 'times per year'. The result depends on the type of industry. It is higher if goods are perishable (e.g. fruit and vegetables) and if consumers make regular purchases (e.g. clothing).

In general, a higher figure is preferable because it means that money is tied up in stock for a shorter time.

■ *TIP* It is possible to convert a stock turnover figure from an annual basis into a daily figure by turning the formula upside-down and multiplying the answer by 365.

stock valuation: procedure for determining the monetary value of a business's *stocks* of raw materials, components, *work-in-progress* and finished goods.

■ Firms are expected to be prudent when valuing their stocks and to undervalue, rather than overvalue them. Firms should take a consistent approach to the valuation of their stock, so that it is easier to compare financial performance over a number of years. There are three main methods: *first in, first out* (FIFO); *last in, first out* (LIFO); and AVCO, which simply uses the average cost of stock purchased as the basis for valuation.

straight-line depreciation: method of writing down the value of an asset over time by removing the same amount of its value each year.

■ This method of *depreciation* is simple to calculate, but might not accurately chart the decline in the value of a *fixed asset* over time. See also *reducing balance method*.

■ *e.g.* This is the calculation of annual depreciation using the straight-line depreciation method for a computer-aided design system that initially cost £100,000 and has a residual value of £40,000 at the end of year 3.

$$\text{annual depreciation} = \frac{\text{cost of asset} - \text{residual value}}{\text{life of asset in years}}$$

$$= \frac{£100,000 - £40,000}{3}$$

$$= £20,000 \text{ per year}$$

strategy: long-term plans through which an organisation aims to attain its *objectives*.

■ If a firm has a long-term objective to maximise its profits, it might do this through strategies such as regular innovation of new products or merging with or taking over rivals. The objective can be viewed as the destination for the firm; the strategy is the means to get to the destination.

structural unemployment: loss of jobs arising from fundamental changes in the economy.

■ Structural unemployment might occur because of technological change or as a result of a permanent change in demand. It is a common phenomenon in most economies and can be difficult to cure as it is often regional in nature and those who become unemployed do not have suitable skills for alternative employment. See also *cyclical unemployment, frictional unemployment* and *seasonal unemployment*.

■ *e.g.* The demand for switchboard operators has declined as a consequence of the development of automated switchboards.

subcontracting: where an individual or organisation passes on some work to a third party.

■ Businesses subcontract their work when they have received more orders than they are capable of supplying, or when they do not possess the specialist skills necessary. Subcontracting assists a business to respond flexibly to fluctuations in demand and avoids the costs of employing additional and specialist staff.

subsidiary: a firm that is owned and controlled by another business, the parent company.

■ If the parent company completely owns the other business (normally holding 100% of its shares), the business is referred to as a wholly owned subsidiary. Subsidiaries differ from divisions or departments within the existing firm in that they operate as entirely separate businesses with their own board of directors and trade under their own name. Subsidiaries are often acquired through *takeovers*.

■ *e.g.* The motor car manufacturer Jaguar is a subsidiary of Ford.

subsidy: financial support provided to an individual, business or industry by the government or other official organisation.

■ Subsidies are used to assist and encourage business activities that are judged essential or desirable. They might be offered in the form of lump-sum grants or price support, whereby a payment is made for each unit of output, allowing subsidised firms to lower their prices. Some subsidies are given in the form of reductions in tax liabilities or by allowing firms to depreciate the cost of assets quickly.

■ *e.g.* In 2000, the government offered an indirect subsidy to small businesses by allowing them to depreciate the cost of purchasing technology (such as computers) in just 1 year. This reduces the tax liability of small firms, providing a real financial benefit.

■ *TIP* Recent governments have made limited use of subsidies, preferring to adopt a more *laissez-faire* approach to the management of the economy.

supervisor: person who oversees the work of other, more junior, employees.

■ Supervisors normally have authority over *shop-floor* employees and report to middle managers in the organisation. Their role has diminished in some firms as greater use has been made of *teamworking* on the shop-floor. Other firms have enhanced the role of supervisors by giving them greater authority. This has permitted the removal of middle managers as part of the process of *delayering*.

supply: quantity of goods and services that a business is willing to sell at any given price over a period of time.

■ A major determinant of supply is the price of the product: higher prices generally attract a greater volume of output. However, for many products, especially agricultural goods, supply is not sensitive to price in the short term.

■ *e.g.* An increase in price will increase the supply of soft fruit only after a sufficient growing period.

■ *TIP* While supply and demand are important in determining price, many candidates waste valuable time in examinations drawing unnecessary demand and supply diagrams. Such diagrams are rarely, if ever, relevant.

supply-side policies: branch of economic theory that advocates the stimulation of *supply* as a means of reducing *unemployment* and *inflation*.

■ In general, supporters of supply-side policies favour minimising government intervention in the economy. Supply-side measures are in direct opposition to the ideas of demand management formulated by John Maynard *Keynes*.

■ *e.g.* Governments use tax cuts and the elimination of barriers to the free working of markets to encourage supply.

■ *TIP* *Privatisation* is another example of the adoption of supply-side policies. One of the main aims of privatising major state-owned businesses was to allow the freer and more efficient operation of markets, thereby encouraging supply.

sweatshop: factory or other working environment where employees are paid very low wages and required to work in crowded, unhealthy conditions.

■ The aim of operating sweatshops is to minimise the costs of production. The implementation of the *minimum wage* in the UK has made sweatshops illegal, but they remain a familiar feature of less economically developed economies.

SWOT analysis: technique used to assess a firm's strengths, weaknesses, opportunities and threats.

■ Strengths and weaknesses relate to a business's internal operation, while opportunities and threats exist in the outside world. A SWOT analysis can be an important stage in the firm developing its business strategy. Managers will aim to build on strengths (e.g. a well-trained workforce) while improving weaknesses (e.g. outdated production equipment). This will enable the business to take advantage of opportunities that exist (e.g. in eastern Europe), while resisting the threat posed by, say, competitors.

takeover: purchase of a controlling interest in one company by another.

▨ This entails the purchase of a minimum of 51% (but usually more) of the shares in the target business. Takeovers can be hostile where the attentions of the predator company are unwelcome and the target company attempts to reject the move. In such circumstances, the predator company only has a certain amount of time to persuade the target's shareholders to accept the offer. Friendly takeovers occur where the target company welcomes the proposed purchase and is likely to recommend the bid to shareholders. Takeovers of companies quoted on the London Stock Exchange are frequently investigated by the *Competition Commission* to confirm that they are in consumers' interests. See also *mergers* and *integration*.

▨ *e.g.* The Bank of Scotland launched a hostile, but ultimately successful bid for the National Westminster Bank in 2000.

tangible assets: items owned by a business that have a physical property.

▨ Tangible assets can take the form of *fixed assets* or *current assets*. Tangible fixed assets are not purchased for resale, but are retained in the business for the purpose of production. See also *intangible assets*.

▨ *e.g.* land, buildings, vehicles and cash.

target market: that part of a *market* (e.g. a segment) to which a business aims to sell its products.

▨ A business will take all its *marketing* decisions with the intention of meeting the needs of its target market. The design of the product, the ways in which it is promoted, its packaging and its price are all selected to meet the needs of its target consumers. Firms sometimes need to change their target market.

▨ *e.g.* The fashion-clothing manufacturer Ellesse targets young people when promoting and selling its products. The **Daily Telegraph**, aware that the segment of the market purchasing its product was steadily ageing, adapted its product and marketing to appeal to younger age groups.

tariff (also called 'import duty' or 'customs duty')**:** tax placed on an imported good or service.

▨ A government might impose tariffs to raise revenue if the *imports* are essential. Alternatively, tariffs might be used to protect home producers from the full

t

force of foreign competition. Opponents of *protectionism* argue that the implementation of tariffs encourages inefficiency among home producers and is therefore not in the public interest. See also *quotas*.

■ *TIP* The UK cannot impose tariffs on imports from other countries in the *European Union* because the Treaty of Rome, which established the EU, created a free trade area between the member states. The EU also operates a common external tariff, which means that imports from countries outside the Union incur the same tariff irrespective of which member state imports them. These tariffs have encouraged many non-EU firms to establish factories in Europe, and the UK has been the most popular location.

taxation: charge imposed by governments, or government agencies, on the trading activities of individuals and organisations.

■ Individuals and businesses are subject to direct taxes (e.g. income tax and corporation tax), which are levied on earnings and profits. The other major category of taxation is indirect taxes, which are taxes on spending. In the UK, the main indirect tax is *value added tax* (VAT). Rates of taxation are an important element in a government's *fiscal policy* and are used to control the economy as well as to promote social justice through the redistribution of income.

Taylor, Frederick: manager and writer who is credited with first developing the science of management.

■ Taylor (1856–1915) was the founder of the *scientific school of management* and a great believer in *mass production* and the *production line*. Taylor observed workers carrying out their duties, and measured and analysed their activities to establish the most efficient methods of completing a task. He then implemented these methods, supervised workers closely and paid *piece-rate* wages. Taylor argued that workers were motivated only by money and that, left unsupervised, they would work at the slowest possible rate. Taylor's ideas were understandably unpopular with employees and vigorously opposed by *trade unions*.

■ *TIP* It is easy to criticise Taylor and to devalue his theories which contrast strongly with those of the *human relations* school of management. However, he should be assessed in the context of his times, and his role in starting the practice of management thinking should not be underestimated.

teamworking: breaking down production into large units and using groups of employees to complete these tasks.

■ Teamworking is intended to increase the *motivation* of employees by offering them greater responsibility, in the expectation of improving their performance. However, the implementation of teamworking requires thorough preparation — not least, *training* for employees who are to take on additional duties. Teamworking is an alternative approach to the division of labour.

■ *e.g.* Teamworking has been used in many businesses in the UK, such as the Honda car factory in Swindon and John Lewis, the retail chain.

■ *TIP* Conventionally, teamworking is presented in a positive light. However, it is not appropriate to all circumstances and managers should compare the costs and benefits before taking a decision. Some major companies have disbanded their team structures because they are judged not to have succeeded.

teleworking: where employees work from home using modern technological forms of communication as a central part of their job.

■ By 1999, approximately 1 million employees in the UK worked from home, although not all teleworkers use technology in their day-to-day work. Firms benefit from reduced costs by employing teleworkers, but a number of major UK businesses have abandoned teleworking after trials.

■ *e.g.* Professionals such as accountants and writers commonly work from home.

■ *TIP* Do not confuse teleworkers and homeworkers. Teleworkers work from home using technology; homeworkers simply work from home and complete non-technological tasks, such as knitting and simple assembly of components.

tertiary sector: that part of the economy comprising businesses engaged in supplying services, such as transport, banking and insurance.

■ The importance of the tertiary sector to the UK economy has increased steadily over the last 50 years. A switch to the production of services (and away from manufacturing) is a feature of an advanced economy. The proportion of the workforce employed in tertiary businesses has also increased, as has the value of services produced. See also *primary sector* and *secondary sector*.

■ By 2000 over two-thirds of the UK's *gross national product* was generated through the supply of services.

test marketing: supply of a new product to a limited geographical area to provide a realistic trial of the product and its *marketing*.

■ Test marketing is intended to answer a number of questions about a product. Crucially, it should provide evidence as to whether the target consumers will, in fact, purchase the product. It shows the likely reaction of retailers to the product and allows an assessment of the effectiveness of the *marketing mix* used. The major drawback of test marketing is that it offers rivals a chance to examine the new product and to prepare their responses prior to the full-scale launch. Most test marketing in the UK is based on regional television areas to limit the extent of advertising.

Theory X: philosophy of *leadership* under which employees are judged to dislike work and to require external control to improve their performance.

■ In 1960, Douglas *McGregor* developed Theory X to describe the traditional 'carrot and stick' approach to managing employees. This assumed that employees were inherently lazy, needed close supervision at all times and worked only to gain money. Theory X advocated the management of employees through coercion, control and direction, and the use of punishment if adequate effort was not made. McGregor lamented that this view of employees influenced managers throughout the USA. See also *Theory Y*.

Theory Y: philosophy of *leadership* that contends that employees enjoy work and regard it as a natural activity.

■ Theory Y assumes that employees seek responsibility and want to use 'imagination, ingenuity and creativity in solving organisational problems'. Douglas *McGregor* supported this view of workers, arguing that the role of a leader should be to develop and liberate the abilities of employees in pursuit of the organisation's objectives. By adopting a Theory Y view of employees, a leader might motivate and improve the performance of the workforce.

■ *TIP* One of the key criticisms of Douglas McGregor's Theory X and Theory Y was that they represented the extremes of leaders' views of their employees. In response to this criticism, McGregor began, before his death in 1964, to develop a new argument: *Theory Z*. William Ouchi developed this work further.

Theory Z: the Japanese approach to the management of people within organisations.

■ William Ouchi suggested that Theory Z comprised a number of features: a commitment to life-long employment; concern for employees, including their social lives; continuous training and appraisal, allied to job security; group-centred working activities; open communication throughout the organisation; worker participation in decision making based on consultation. Ouchi argued that any firm managing its workers according to these principles would benefit in terms of employee performance.

time management: series of techniques designed to enable employees to make the most effective use of the time available at the workplace.

■ *e.g.* prioritising tasks, controlling the duration of conversations and eliminating unnecessary activities.

time series analysis: forecasting technique that finds a pattern or *trend* in historical data and uses this as a basis for future projections.

■ Time series analysis is used on various types of data, including those relating to sales, production and prices. If a pattern is discovered, this can be used to forecast future behaviour. Time series analysis attempts to discover: long-term trends (are the data rising or falling?); cyclical and seasonal fluctuations (are there regular, periodic fluctuations in the data?); and random changes (how do random, non-recurring events, e.g. political unrest in a foreign market, affect the data?). Once these patterns have been analysed, it is possible to forecast the data into the future. The major weakness of time series analysis is that it assumes that the past is an accurate basis for forecasting the future.

total quality management (TQM): approach to management that places responsibility for the quality of work in the hands of all employees within the organisation.

■ Under TQM, products are constantly monitored as they pass through the production process. Each area or department in a firm is viewed as a customer or supplier and will not accept *work-in-progress* that does not conform to agreed quality standards. Causes of errors and defects are investigated, identified and eliminated. The implementation of TQM requires a change in the *culture* of an organisation so that all employees accept an individual and collective responsibility for maintaining high standards of quality. TQM aims to prevent defects rather than to cure them once they have occurred. By reducing the proportion of defective products, TQM can provide a firm with an important competitive advantage.

■ *TIP* TQM is really an advanced form of customer orientation. It operates with the fundamental idea that all employees have a relationship with the customer.

TQM: see *total quality management*.

trade credit: period of grace offered by suppliers before payment for goods or services is due.

■ In effect, trade credit is a short-term loan offered free of any interest charges. This can be an important source of short-term finance for many businesses, improving their *cash flow*. However, some businesses make trade credit less attractive by offering discounts for early payment.

■ *TIP* It is one of the ironies of the business world that the organisations that need trade credit most find it difficult to obtain. New businesses and those in a poor financial position would benefit from being given time to pay accounts, but suppliers are likely to demand early settlement of their accounts because of the risk of non-payment.

trade cycle: see *business cycle*.

trade mark: striking and recognisable name, logo or symbol that identifies a business, product or *brand*.

■ Trade marks are valuable properties, as organisations invest considerable resources in developing them and establishing them in the minds of consumers. Since the Trades Marks Act 1994, the definition of trade marks has been extended to include smells, sounds, the shape of products and their packaging as well as brand names and logos.

■ *e.g.* Perrier can prevent other firms from copying its distinctive bottle and Nestlé is able to protect the unusual triangular shape of its Toblerone chocolate bar.

Trades Union Congress (TUC): federation of over 70 *trade unions* in the UK.

■ Founded in Manchester in 1868, the TUC carries out a number of functions in the business environment. It brings unions together to draw up common policies on employment law, ways of tackling unemployment and other workplace issues as well as lobbying the government to implement policies that will benefit people at work, such as the *minimum wage*. Above all, the TUC campaigns for fairness and justice for all employees in the workplace. TUC policy is set by the annual Congress, which meets for 4 days of debate each year in early September.

trade union: organisation of workers formed with the aim of protecting and enhancing the economic position and working conditions of its members.

■ Various types of trade union exist, including *general unions, industrial unions* and occupational unions. Unions engage in *collective bargaining* with management to negotiate pay and working conditions (e.g. the number of days' holiday to which employees are entitled) and to improve job security. During the 1980s and 1990s, membership of trade unions declined steadily, although there has been an upturn recently.

■ *e.g.* The UK's largest union is UNISON with a membership in excess of 1 million.

■ *TIP* The distinction between the various types of union has tended to blur and general unions have become more important.

trade union legislation: series of Acts of Parliament passed to regulate the activities of *trade unions* and the actions of their members.

■ Conservative governments in the 1980s and 1990s passed the principal Acts constraining trade union activity. The major pieces of legislation are the Employment Acts of 1980, 1982, 1988 and 1990, the Trade Union Act 1984 and the Trade Union Reform and Employment Rights Act 1993. This legislation outlawed *closed shops*, controlled the extent of *picketing* and made secret ballots before strike action mandatory.

trading profit: see *operating profit*.

training: provision of job-related skills and knowledge.

■ Training can give a business a competitive advantage through the possession of a more productive workforce that produces a minimal number of defective products. Training can be *on-the-job*, at the place of work, or *off-the-job*, at a local college or other training centre.

transfer pricing: charging policy used to determine the rates paid for materials, components and finished goods when traded between different elements of the same organisation.

■ Transfer prices operate in relation to deals between different parts of the same business operating within a single country. In addition, some *multinationals* manipulate their transfer prices to minimise tax payments, by ensuring that they have low tax liability in those countries with high rates of *taxation*.

■ *e.g.* If Vauxhall imports engines from Australia for use in its Luton factory, an agreed transfer price will be paid by the UK assembly factory to the Australian manufacturing plant.

Treasury: government department responsible for managing the public finances.

■ The Treasury oversees the collection of *taxation* and *public* spending. It operates with the aims of raising the rate of sustainable growth and achieving rising prosperity through the creation of economic and employment opportunities for all. The work of the Treasury is under the direction of the *Chancellor of the Exchequer*.

trend: underlying pattern of growth or decline in a series of data.

■ Identifying the trend in data can help businesses to forecast the future.

■ *e.g.* In the diagram below, the trend is used to forecast future sales.

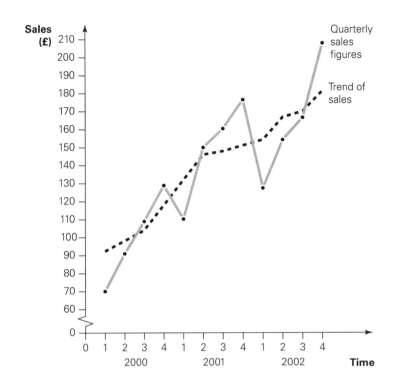

turnover: value of total sales achieved by a business during an *accounting period*.

■ A business's turnover figure is recorded on its *profit and loss account*.

■ *TIP* The term 'turnover' is used in other contexts in business studies. It can relate to the number of times a firm's average stock is sold annually and the proportion of its labour force leaving during a year.

two-way communication: the exchange of information and ideas up and down the organisational hierarchy.

■ This type of *communication* is associated with *democratic leadership* (perhaps within a delayered *organisational structure*), offering employees a considerable role in the decision-making process. It allows employees the opportunity to put forward ideas and to provide *feedback* to communication received from those higher in the organisation. Two-way communication is essential for the operation of techniques designed to improve employee *motivation* (e.g. *delegation*).

ultimate consumer (also called 'end user'): person or organisation that buys and uses a product in its final form.

■ The ultimate consumer is the last point in the process of production, which in the case of manufacturing might begin with the extraction of materials and pass through several manufacturing stages.

under-utilised capacity: see *excess capacity*.

underwriting: process by which a financial institution agrees to purchase any unsold *shares* following a share issue.

■ Merchant banks normally provide the service of underwriting. In return for a fee, the institution accepts the risk of purchasing unsold shares at a price below the initial sale price. The company issuing the shares has the security of knowing that it will sell all the shares in the issue for a minimum amount.

■ *TIP* Underwriting has a more general meaning in relation to taking on risk. Thus, insurance companies are underwriters, taking all the risk of compensating for fire, accident or theft in return for a premium.

unemployment: number of people seeking a job who are unable to find one.

■ Unemployment is normally expressed as a straightforward figure (e.g. 1 million) or as a percentage of the labour force. It represents an enormous waste of a society's productive resources and most governments aim to maintain it at the lowest possible level. A number of types of unemployment exist. Regional unemployment measures the rates effective in various parts of the UK. *Structural unemployment* arises from fundamental changes in the economy (e.g. technological change). *Seasonal unemployment* occurs at particular times of the year and is common in certain industries (e.g. agriculture). *Frictional unemployment* is normal in a healthy economy and results from people changing jobs.

unfair dismissal: termination of a worker's contract of employment without good reason. Under *employment protection legislation,* employees may only be dismissed for certain specified reasons: genuine *redundancy*, where a job no longer exists; gross misconduct (e.g. theft of the employer's property or an act of violence in the workplace); inadequate performance, meaning that the employee cannot satisfactorily complete his or her duties; another substantial reason (e.g. the ending of a temporary contract). Any other reason for dismissal is unfair. Employees who believe that they have been unfairly dismissed can claim compensation by taking their case to an *industrial tribunal*.

- *TIP* There is some confusion between unfair dismissal and *constructive dismissal*. Constructive dismissal occurs when an employer behaves in such a way that an employee feels forced to leave his or her job.

unincorporated: status of a business in which the owners are not legally distinct from the business itself.

- Where the business is not a separate legal entity from its owners, the owners are responsible for the full amount of any debts incurred by the business. See also *unlimited liability*.
- *e.g.* *sole traders* and *partnerships*.

union recognition: where the management of a business acknowledges the right of a particular *trade union* to negotiate on behalf of its members.

- If a union is not recognised, its actions might be illegal. Managers do not have to recognise a union for the purpose of *collective bargaining*, but recognition can offer advantages for a business. Communication with employees becomes simpler and negotiations might be easier to conduct when undertaken with a small group of experienced employees.
- *TIP* It is easy to assume that firms would benefit from not recognising unions. The workforce would be less organised and pay rates might be lower. However, the presence of unions in the workforce offers benefits in terms of communication, employee morale and the monitoring of health and safety.

unique selling proposition (or 'point') **(USP):** feature or factor that differentiates a business's product from those supplied by its competitors.

- Once a business has identified the USP associated with its product, it will normally use this as the basis of its *promotion*. Creating a USP can assist a business in developing *brand loyalty* for its products and might make demand for the product more price inelastic, allowing the firm to charge higher prices without significant loss of sales.
- *e.g.* The Co-operative Bank has created a unique selling proposition by adopting an ethical stance. This has been at the heart of much of its subsequent marketing activities.
- *TIP* Having a USP is particularly important in industries where the firms sell products that are perceived as similar. Thus, brewers of beer emphasise, for example, the smoothness or strength of their particular product.

unissued capital: *shares* that a company is legally entitled to sell, but has not yet issued.

- The amount of shares that a company intends to issue is stated in its *Memorandum of Association* and is termed its *authorised share capital*. However, these might not all be issued at the time of the company's formation. The balance withheld is unissued capital.

unit cost (also called 'average cost'): average level of expenses incurred in producing a single item of a good or service.

▧ The unit cost is calculated by dividing the total cost of production by the number of units of output. It tends to fall initially as output increases, owing to *economies of scale*. As output continues to rise, *diseconomies of scale* come into operation, resulting in a rise in average cost. Together these factors create the U-shaped curve illustrated below.

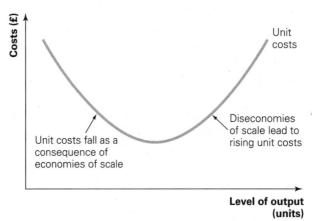

▧ *TIP* The level of unit cost has important implications for a firm's *pricing method*. Unit costs might also provide a motive for growth by *merger* or *takeover*.

unlimited liability: where the responsibility of the owners of a business for the debts of the enterprise is not restricted in any way.

▧ Unlimited liability applies to the owners of *unincorporated* businesses, such as *partnerships* and *sole traders*. In the circumstances of unlimited liability, the owners of an enterprise might have to sell personal possessions to settle the business's debts. See also *limited liability*.

Unlisted Securities Market (USM): a parallel *Stock Exchange* established in 1980 to provide a market for smaller companies to sell their shares.

▧ This market offered smaller companies (which were unable to get a listing on the full Stock Exchange) an opportunity to raise capital through the issue of *shares*. The USM was not successful and in 1996 it was discontinued; the *Alternative Investment Market* took over its role.

unofficial strike: decision by workers to withdraw their labour that has not been organised or approved by the relevant *trade union*.

▧ Unofficial or 'wildcat' strikes were common in the UK in the 1970s, but they declined thereafter. This was due principally to *trade union legislation* making employees vulnerable to legal action by employers for undertaking strike action not ratified by the trade union.

▧ *TIP* The UK's improved industrial relations record (as shown by the reduction in unofficial strikes) has been a major factor encouraging the location of foreign firms (e.g. Nissan and Honda) in the country.

USM: see *Unlisted Securities Market*.

USP: see *unique selling proposition*.

utilities: companies providing supplies of gas, water and electricity to businesses and private homes.

■ Utilities in the UK used to be state-owned but were sold to private owners as part of the policy of *privatisation*. They make an important contribution to the economy. By operating efficiently and providing their products at the lowest possible prices, they contribute to the *international competitiveness* of UK businesses.

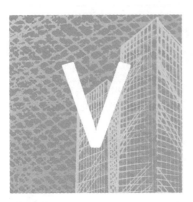

vacancy: an unfilled job for which no employee is currently available.

■ The level of vacancies is an important indicator of the state of the economy. During the boom stage of the *business cycle*, the number of vacancies rises. The opposite is true during a *slump*.

■ *TIP* It might seem strange that an economy can have *unemployment* and vacancies at the same time. The reason why they can co-exist is that the available jobs and the unemployed people might be in different parts of the country. Alternatively, those who are unemployed might not have the correct skills to take up the vacant positions, or may be unaware of the jobs.

value added: difference between the revenue earned by a business and the costs incurred in production, such as expenditure on raw materials, components, labour services and overheads.

■ Value is added to goods and services through the processes of *production* and *marketing*. A firm that has annual sales of £100 million and expenditure of £75 million on raw materials, components and bought-in services would generate a value added of £25 million. See also *value added tax*.

■ *e.g.* Businesses selling mineral water have been able to charge relatively high prices (thereby adding value) as a result of clever marketing that emphasises its superiority over tap water.

value added tax (VAT): indirect tax levied on businesses according to the value they add during the process of *production*.

■ Businesses pay VAT on the goods and services they purchase and, if registered for the tax, they levy VAT on the goods and services they sell. Customs and Excise collects the difference between the amount of VAT a firm levies and the amount it pays. Ultimately, VAT is charged on the final selling price of the product and the consumer bears this cost. Not all goods and services in the UK are liable for VAT: some goods are exempt, such as newspapers.

■ *TIP* VAT is a bureaucratic tax to operate and imposes a considerable administrative burden on businesses, especially smaller ones. Because of this, businesses with a turnover of less than £52,000 (in 2000/01) do not have to register for the tax and are not required to charge it on products that they sell.

value analysis: technique for evaluating the effectiveness of producing a product.

▓ Value analysis aims to achieve a product that will continue to meet the requirements of customers, but at a lower cost. It might result in the redesign of a product, the alteration of the manufacturing process, or finding an improved and more cost-effective source of supply.

▓ *e.g.* Value analysis of a greenhouse might indicate that the panes of glass can be held in place with metal clips, rather than traditional putty. This might reduce the costs of manufacturing and assembly without affecting the function of the greenhouse.

▓ *TIP* Value analysis is particularly applicable in the context of *mass production*. A small saving in the manufacturing cost of a single item of production can enhance profits significantly when received on millions of units of output.

variable costs: those expenses incurred by a business that increase directly with the volume of output.

▓ The diagram below shows the relationships that might exist between the volume of production and the cost of items classified as variable costs.

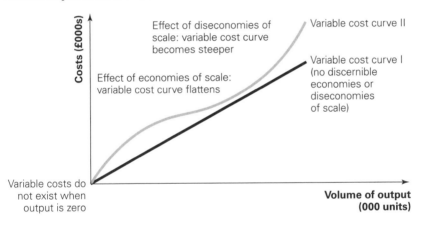

▓ *e.g.* expenditure on fuel, shop-floor labour, components and raw materials.

▓ *TIP* Don't automatically assume that variable costs rise steadily with the volume of output, as illustrated in curve I above. The effects of *economies of scale* and *diseconomies of scale* might produce a variable cost curve such as curve II. See also *fixed costs* and *semi-variable costs*.

variable overheads: expenses classified as *overheads* that increase directly with the volume of output.

▓ *e.g.* The commission paid to a business's sales force might be a variable overhead, since it is a cost not directly associated with a particular product, but will increase along with the volume of output.

variance: difference between expected (or budgeted) costs, revenues and profits and the actual figures.

▓ Variances are described as 'favourable' if costs are lower than expected, or revenues or profits are higher than anticipated; or as 'adverse' when costs are higher than budgeted, or revenues or profits lower than forecast.

e.g. The following table shows examples of favourable and adverse variances.

Revenue/cost	Budgeted figure (£)	Actual figure (£)	Variance (£)	
Income from sales	195,000	202,000	7,000	favourable
Expenses				
Labour	55,000	58,000	(3,000)	adverse
Raw materials and fuel	60,000	58,500	1,500	favourable
Rent and rates	48,000	48,000	0	no variance
Total costs	163,000	164,500	(1,500)	adverse
Profit	32,000	37,500	5,500	favourable

TIP When analysing variances, never simply describe the data. Examiners do not award marks for this. Concentrate on the causes and effects of variances, considering those examples where the variance is greatest.

VAT: see *value added tax*.

venture capital (also called 'risk capital'): funds advanced to organisations judged to be relatively high risk, in the form of *share capital* and *loan capital*.

■ The provision of venture capital is a large and growing business: the UK venture capital industry has invested over £35 billion in approximately 19,000 companies since 1983. Financial institutions (e.g. merchant banks) provide venture capital, as do individuals known as *business angels*. Organisations and individuals providing venture capital frequently want some control over the organisation for which they are providing finance. Owners might need to sell some *shares* in their companies (generally a minority stake) to the venture backer, who might seek a *non-executive director* role and attend monthly board meetings. Venture capital investors provide not only *equity capital*, but also experience, contacts and advice when required. These features distinguish venture capital from other *sources of finance*.

■ **TIP** Providers of venture capital will not advance huge amounts to businesses. It is unusual for venture capitalists to lend in excess of £500,000 in a single deal.

verbal communication: exchange of information and ideas by word of mouth.

■ Verbal communication provides rapid *feedback* and, if it allows those communicating to see each other, it can provide additional information through body language and facial expressions. Verbal communication is appropriate when dealing with sensitive situations such as making an employee redundant. However, it does not normally provide a permanent record and typically participants remember only about 30% of a conversation. See also *communication*.

■ **e.g.** face-to-face, by telephone or through the use of video conferencing systems. Verbal communication is used in businesses in presentations, meetings and interviews.

■ **TIP** Try to avoid saying that a particular form of communication is good or bad. A stronger line of argument is to note the circumstances in which a particular form is appropriate or inappropriate.

vertical communication: exchange of information and ideas between people at different levels in an organisation.

■ Vertical communication is likely to be more effective if it is two-way: that is, if subordinates are encouraged to communicate with those further up the organisational hierarchy and to respond to downward communication. See also *feedback* and *communication*.

■ *e.g.* a director sending a memo to a middle manager or a supervisor issuing instructions to a shop-floor worker.

vertical integration: bringing together two or more businesses in the same industry but at different stages of production.

■ This type of *integration* offers a number of benefits to businesses, including certainty of supplies and the provision of outlets for products. However, as with *horizontal integration*, it can be subject to investigation by the *Competition Commission* if considered to be against the public interest.

■ *e.g.* In 2000, BUPA, the private care provider, purchased 28.5% of the shares in the Communities Hospitals Group. This gave the company a series of outlets for its health care provision.

video conferencing: transmission of sound and pictures allowing communication between people in different locations.

■ The system is interactive and operates through computer link-ups. Time and travelling costs can be saved by using video conferencing. It is particularly popular with multinational companies, where employees might be thousands of kilometres apart.

visible trade: exchange of goods (and not services) across national frontiers.

■ *e.g.* the purchase of Belgian chocolate by UK retailers; the sale of Scotch whisky to importers in the USA.

voluntary code of practice: guidelines relating to a range of business activities recommended by the government and other organisations.

■ Voluntary codes of practice have no legal authority and cannot be enforced in a court of law. However, in the event of businesses repeatedly ignoring voluntary codes of practice, it is likely that the government would enact appropriate legislation.

■ *e.g.* The *Advertising Standards Authority* established and oversees a number of codes of practice in relation to advertising. The chemical industry's code of practice, 'Responsible Care Programme', arose from of a series of high-profile chemical disasters that eroded public confidence in the industry.

voluntary liquidation: dissolution of a company through the sale of its *assets* and the settling of its *liabilities* at the request of the directors or shareholders.

■ A liquidator arranges for the company's assets to be sold and oversees the process. Any money raised by the sale of assets is shared among the company's *creditors* according to an agreed formula. If there are insufficient funds, creditors receive a set proportion of what they are owed, although certain creditors such as the Inland Revenue are given preference. See also *liquidation*.

wage inflation: sustained rise in the general level of prices caused by the increasing cost of labour services.

■ As *wages* and *salaries* form about 65% of production costs in the UK, prices set by businesses are sensitive to increases in labour costs. In recent years, legislation has been passed to restrict *trade union* power with the aim of reducing the inflationary impetus arising from increasing wages and salaries. Controlling wage rises and hence prices is an important element in improving *international competitiveness*.

wages: money paid to an employee for his or her labour services, normally expressed as a weekly figure.

■ It is common for wages to be linked to employees working a specific number of hours and they might be stated in terms of an hourly rate. Wages are normally paid weekly and are the usual form of remuneration for manual workers and *shop-floor* employees. Wages can be gross (before the deduction of taxes and national insurance) or net (after deductions have taken place). See also *salary*.

walkout: where an organisation's employees stop working and leave their place of employment as a protest.

■ Walkouts are a tactic used by employees during an *industrial dispute*. *Trade union legislation* has made it illegal for a union to organise a spontaneous walkout.

wealth: the total value of the *assets* of a nation, business or individual.

■ Wealth is a stock or store of value, whereas *income* represents a flow taking place over time. Wealth can be divided into personal wealth (possessions such as property and furniture owned by people), business wealth (an organisation's total assets, whether tangible or intangible) and social wealth (assets owned by the state, such as roads, schools and hospitals).

weighted average: an *average* of a number of items, some of which are given more or less importance within the calculation.

■ By weighting the data to reflect the relative importance of the components, it is possible to calculate a final average that is meaningful.

■ *e.g.* Suppose a business employs three grades of employees as shown below.

Employee	No. of employees	Annual salary
Grade A	600	£15,000
Grade B	300	£21,000
Grade C	100	£30,000

A simple answer to the question 'What is the average wage paid by the business?' would be £15,000 + £21,000 + £30,000 divided by 3 = £66,000/3 = £22,000. However, this is not representative of the typical wage paid by the organisation because the majority of its employees earn only £15,000. Calculating a weighted average, taking into account the proportions of employees receiving the various salaries, would produce a more meaningful result.

No. of employees	Employee salary	×	Weight	=	Weighted total
600	£15,000	×	60	=	900,000
300	£21,000	×	30	=	630,000
100	£30,000	×	10	=	300,000
			100		1,830,000

The weighted average is calculated by dividing the sum of the weighted totals by the total of the weights (1,830,000/100) = £18,300. This figure is a more accurate indicator of the wages typically paid in the above example and somewhat lower than the simple average.

weighted index: calculation of an *index number*, based on the figure 100, in which the procedures used for a *weighted average* are applied.

■ The best-known weighted index in the UK is the *retail price index*. In this index, the weights attached to the importance of various goods and services are in proportion to the amount spent on them by consumers.

whistle blower: someone in an organisation who tells the authorities or the media that something illegal or unethical is taking place.

■ Following a number of accidents involving public transport, airline and railway employees were urged by MPs and the media to act as informers and report any fears concerning safety matters. Over recent years, whistle blowing has attracted considerable attention from the media. Some employers have threatened employees with disciplinary action or even dismissal if they reveal undesirable activities to outside parties.

■ *TIP* In July 1999, the Public Interest Disclosure Act came into force to provide protection for informers. The Act protects employees who are sacked or victimised for making a disclosure about criminal offences, breaches of legal obligation, miscarriages of justice, health and safety dangers and environmental risk. There is provision in the legislation for unlimited compensation for dismissal.

white-collar union: organisation of workers formed to protect and enhance the economic position and working conditions of non-manual workers.

▪ White-collar unions represent clerical, administrative and professional employees. They have a reputation for being less militant than some other types of union. See also *trade union* and *general union*.

▪ *e.g.* Association of University Teachers and National Union of Journalists.

white knight company: company that purchases *shares* in another that is threatened by a hostile *takeover*.

▪ A white knight company normally purchases enough shares in the threatened business to prevent the hostile takeover from occurring. The target company usually welcomes the attentions of the white knight company.

wholesale cooperative: organisation that supplies goods and services to its members and other *cooperative* organisations.

▪ This form of wholesaling operates on typical cooperative principles: the organisation is managed by its members or customers, and any profits are shared between the members according to the amount of stock they have purchased.

▪ *e.g.* In the UK, the Co-operative Wholesale Society supplies products to cooperative shops throughout the country.

wholesaler: organisation that purchases goods for the purpose of resale.

▪ A wholesaler normally purchases products in bulk and receives a discount in return for the size of the order. Wholesalers sell their products to retailers in smaller quantities. They sometimes provide advice and technical support to retailers and might also offer them credit terms.

▪ *TIP* The importance of the wholesaler in the process of *distribution* is declining. Some retailers (especially food retailers) are performing the role of wholesaler as well as retailer and enjoying increased *profit margins* as a consequence.

winding up: see *liquidation*.

window dressing: construction of financial documents in order to present a company's performance in the best possible light.

▪ Managers sometimes improve the cash position revealed by a *balance sheet* through delaying the payment of bills or bringing forward sales into an earlier trading period. Equally, businesses occasionally sell fixed assets (and lease them back) immediately before the end of the financial year to enhance holdings of cash on their published accounts. Businesses can also improve their financial position by altering their *depreciation* policy and reducing the value of their assets on the balance sheet more slowly. This increases the profits recorded on the *profit and loss account* and the value of the business's assets shown on the balance sheet.

▪ *TIP* Does window dressing work? Due to the publicity given to cases of window dressing in the media, investors are more aware of the methods used by businesses to enhance their apparent financial position. If companies are to continue to present their accounts in the best possible light, new techniques of window dressing might need to be used.

worker participation: involvement of employees in decision-making activities within the organisation.

■ Worker participation might entail the use of *quality circles* and *works councils* to provide a forum for employees' views. Worker participation tends to be less formal in approach than *industrial democracy*, but is also intended to motivate employees.

workers' cooperative: a form of organisation whereby workers own and manage the enterprise in which they work.

■ There are no outside owners, although there might be managers in a large firm; all the employees have the right to be members and take decisions about the cooperative at regular meetings. In a workers' cooperative, ownership of the business is restricted to the employees. This means that members/workers, rather than outsiders, make the decisions about the running of the cooperative. Cooperatives can use advisers and consultants, but the real control is in the hands of the employees.

■ *e.g.* In the UK there are over 1,500 workers' cooperatives in many fields, including building, catering, computers, dressmaking and high-tech industries.

■ *TIP* In spite of their shortcomings, the number of workers' cooperatives is rising in the UK. This form of business organisation is encouraged and supported by the Co-operative Development Agency (CDA).

working capital (also called 'net current assets'): a business's *current assets* less its *current liabilities*.

■ Working capital is important to businesses, as without a surplus of current assets over current liabilities, they might be unable to meet their financial obligations. Businesses can be short of working capital during periods of growth, when they face increased costs for additional raw materials and labour: this is known as *overtrading*. Working capital is also called *net current assets* and is shown on a company's *balance sheet*.

■ *TIP* Some businesses (e.g. retailers) might operate with low levels of working capital because their customers settle their accounts immediately.

working conditions: the environment in which employees carry out their duties and the regulations that relate to their employment.

■ Working conditions can have a profound impact on the performance of employees and are subject to negotiation through the process of *collective bargaining*.

■ *e.g.* the warmth and cleanliness of the workplace, the provision of rest areas and leisure facilities, hours of work and holiday entitlement.

work-in-progress: goods that are still in the process of *production*.

■ It is usual for work-in-progress to be included in *stock valuation*, although its value might vary according to the system used.

■ *e.g.* incomplete goods on the production line of a manufacturing business.

works council: forum within a business where employees and management meet to discuss issues such as pay and *working conditions*.

Employee representatives on a works council are normally elected. Works councils offer an opportunity for *consultation* to take place and might be independent of any negotiations undertaken by *trade unions*. It is common for works councils to be used in workplaces where no trade union representation exists.

work study: analysis of the ways in which employees carry out particular duties.

Work study compares existing and new methods of work and measures the time taken by a skilled employee to complete a given duty using a variety of approaches. It is a central feature of the *scientific school of management* and is used to decide on techniques that make the most effective use of employees. See also Frederick *Taylor*.

work-to-rule: form of protest by employees in which work is completed more slowly than normal by precisely following the terms of their contracts and *job descriptions*.

This results in a less flexible labour force and lower levels of productivity, but does not infringe the contract of employment or give employers a reason not to pay wages. It might lead to employees requiring greater supervision, as they might be less willing to take on responsibilities not stated in their contracts of employment. A work-to-rule might be followed by strike action if the former tactic does not place the employer under sufficient pressure.

world-class manufacturing: series of techniques designed to satisfy the customer totally by producing high-quality goods and services at the right price and supplied on time.

To become world-class manufacturers, businesses must operate at standards equal to the best in the world. Companies that fall into this category hold limited levels of *stocks*, reduce manufacturing *lead time*, introduce new products frequently, keep costs to a minimum and produce very few faulty products. See also *benchmarking*.

World Wide Web: system for browsing *Internet* sites, so called because it is made of many sites linked together.

Technically, the Web is a global (worldwide) system that enables the navigation of Internet sites. It was created at a research institute in Switzerland in 1989. Users can travel from one site to another using browsers like Netscape Navigator and Internet Explorer. Incorporating hypermedia (graphics, sounds, animations and video), the Web has become the ideal medium for publishing information on the Internet. The commercial possibilities of the Web are enormous and are attracting considerable attention from businesses and the media.

x-inefficiency: when a business produces a product at a higher cost than might be the case in other circumstances.

■ *e.g.* Monopolies are often accused of being x-inefficient and this is one of the possible reasons for their investigation by the *Competition Commission*.

year (financial): the 12 months over which a business calculates its accounts.

■ It is common for businesses to conclude their financial year on 31 March (to tie in with the fiscal year) or on 31 December (to match the calendar year). See also *year (fiscal)*.

■ *TIP* Businesses can trade for a period in excess of 1 year before producing financial statements. When analysing accounts (and especially turnover figures), check the period to which the data relate. See also *accounting period*.

year (fiscal): the 12-month period used by the government and its agencies for calculating financial matters.

■ One of the most important organisations using the fiscal year (6 April to the following 5 April) is the Inland Revenue. Companies have their tax liabilities assessed over the fiscal year, rather than their own financial year. In addition, the government plans its own spending over the fiscal year. In effect, the fiscal year is the government's financial year. See also *year (financial)*.

year end: end of the financial year for a business.

■ This is the time at which financial statements are constructed and judgements can be made about the performance of the business in comparison to previous financial years. See also *year (financial)*.

yield: return on an *investment*, expressed as a percentage.

■ This term is particularly used in relation to the return on investments in financial securities such as *stocks* and *shares*. A commonly used measure is the *dividend yield*, which expresses the dividend earned on shares as a percentage of the current market price of the share.

■ *TIP* Yields are important because they allow comparisons to be made on the returns gained (or expected) from competing investments. Remember, however, that risk plays a role here and should be included as part of any comparison. A risky investment should provide a higher yield.

X y Z

zero budgets: a system whereby *budgets* are automatically set at zero and those responsible for them have to argue a case to receive any funds.

■ Zero budgets are used in an attempt to control costs. Zero budgeting can result in the most articulate or forceful managers receiving the highest budgets, irrespective of need. One alternative is to allow budget holders the same amount of money as in the previous year, plus an adjustment for inflation and other circumstances. In these circumstances, a business's costs can continually rise.

zero defects: quality system that aims for perfection, making no allowance for faulty products.

■ Most firms recognise that perfection is not attainable, but by stating it as an aim, they expect to reduce the number of defects to 'parts per million' (e.g. five defects per million products). Reducing the proportion of defects assists in controlling costs by reducing the number of items that are scrapped or reworked. It also improves customers' perceptions of the organisation and might allow a premium price to be charged.

zero hours contract: highly flexible form of employment contract under which the employer does not guarantee to provide work and pays only for work actually done.

■ The number of hours worked by the employee will vary according to the level of demand experienced by the business and the availability of other workers. Work carried out by workers on zero hours contracts tends to be low-skilled and includes occupation groups such as clerical workers, sales representatives, delivery drivers and packing staff. Since 1994, those working on zero hours contracts have been entitled to the same benefits as other part-time employees.

Key AS terms

Marketing

above the line
adding value
advertising
advertising elasticity
Advertising Standards
   Authority
below the line
Boston matrix
brand
brand leader
brand loyalty
consumer
consumer durable
corporate image
customer service
demand
desk research
direct mail
direct response marketing
disposable income
distribution
distribution channels
e-commerce
field research
hypermarket
impulse purchases
loss leader
market
market-based pricing
marketing

marketing mix
marketing model
marketing objectives
market niche
market orientation
market penetration
market price
market research
market segmentation
market share
mark-up
merchandising
'me too' product
niche marketing
own-brand products
packaging
penetration pricing
persuasive advertising
place
point-of-sale
predatory pricing
press release
price discrimination
price skimming
price taker
price transparency
price war
pricing strategies
pricing tactics
primary data

primary research
product design
product development
product differentiation
product life cycle
product orientation
product portfolio
promotion
psychological pricing
public relations
qualitative research
quantitative research
questionnaire
quota sample
random sample
retail audit
sales promotion
sales revenue
sales volume
sampling
secondary data
secondary research
social class
sponsorship
supply
test marketing
unique selling
   proposition (USP)
value added

Finance and accounting

absorption costing
accounting period
annual report and
   accounts
asset
average costs
average fixed costs
balance sheet
bankruptcy

break even
budgeting
budgets
business angel
capital
capital budget
cash flow
cash-flow forecast
contribution

contribution costing
cost
cost centre
current assets
debenture
debtor
direct cost
external financing
factoring

fixed assets
fixed costs
full costing
hire purchase
indirect costs
invoice
liabilities
liquidity
loss
margin of safety
mortgage
net cash flow
operating profit

overdraft
overheads
overtrading
ploughed-back profit
profit
profit and loss account
profit centre
profit margin
retained profit
revenue budget
sale and leaseback
semi-variable costs
share

shareholder
sources of finance
tangible assets
trading profit
unit cost
variable costs
variable overheads
variance
working capital
year (financial)
year (fiscal)
zero budgets

Operations management

batch production
benchmarking
bottlenecks
buffer stock
bulk buying
capacity
capacity shortage
capacity utilisation
capital intensive
cell production
computer-aided design
computer-aided
   manufacture
continuous improvement
copyright
downtime
economic order quantity
economies of scale

efficiency
excess capacity
factors of production
flexible specialisation
flow production
innovation
Japanisation
just-in-time
kaizen
kanban
labour intensive
lead time
lean production
mass production
overcapacity
patent
performance indicators
production

production line
productivity
quality assurance
quality circle
quality control
reorder level
research and development
scale
simultaneous engineering
single sourcing
stock
stock control
stock rotation
subcontracting
total quality management
under-utilised capacity
zero defects

People and organisations

Advisory, Conciliation and
   Arbitration Service
autonomous working
   group
binding arbitration
centralisation
communication
conciliation
consultation
decentralisation
delayering

delegation
democratic leadership
empowerment
expectancy theory
flexible working
fringe benefits
Hawthorne effect
headhunter
health and safety
Herzberg, Frederick
hierarchy of needs

human relations
human resource
   management
hygiene
industrial democracy
job description
job design
job enlargement
job enrichment
job evaluation
job rotation

job specification
labour market
labour mobility
laissez-faire
leadership
line manager
McGregor, Douglas
management by objectives
manpower planning
Maslow, Abraham
matrix management
Mayo, Elton
minimum wage
motivation

off-the-job training
organisational structure
overtime
paternalistic leadership
   style
performance-related pay
peripheral workers
personnel management
piece-rate pay
quality circle
salary
scientific school of
   management
self-employed

span of control
supervisor
teamworking
Theory X
Theory Y
trade union
vacancy
wages
worker participation
work study

The business environment

balance of payments
balance of trade
Bank of England
bank rate
barriers to entry
business cycle
cartel
Chancellor of the
   Exchequer
civil law
collusion
Companies Act
Competition Commission
competition policy
consumer protection
   legislation
cyclical unemployment

economic growth
exchange rate
Fair Trading Act
fiscal policy
frictional unemployment
imports
information technology
interest rate
macroeconomics
mixed economy
monetary policy
monopolies and mergers
   legislation
monopoly
national income
newly industrialised
   country

Office of Fair Trading
private sector
privatisation
public spending
quota
recession
restrictive practice
seasonal unemployment
single European
   currency
slump
stakeholder
structural unemployment
tertiary sector
unemployment
voluntary code
   of practice

Objectives and strategy

Articles of Association
board of directors
business plan
capital
cash flow
cash-flow forecast
collateral
company
cooperative
copyright
corporate objectives

deed of partnership
desk research
director
divorce of ownership from
   control
entrepreneur
external financing
field research
free enterprise
growth
holding company

incorporation
innovation
insolvency
investment
laissez-faire
limited liability
loan capital
location
management
market
market research

Memorandum of
  Association
mission statement
non-executive director
non-profit-making
  organisation
objectives
opportunity cost
overtrading
partnership
patent
ploughed-back profit

primary sector
private limited company
private sector
product design
profit
public limited company
Registrar of Companies
research and development
secondary sector
sleeping partner
sources of finance
stakeholder

Stock Exchange
subsidiary
SWOT analysis
tertiary sector
unincorporated
unlimited liability
Unlisted Securities Market
venture capital
wholesale cooperative
workers' cooperative
working capital